SANDHILL SUNDAYS
AND OTHER
RECOLLECTIONS

Sandhill Sundays

and other recollections

MARI SANDOZ

University of Nebraska Press　·　Lincoln

Publishers on the Plains

UNP

Copyright 1930 by North American Review, Inc.
Copyright 1931, 1933, 1952 by Mari Sandoz
Copyright 1936 by Curtis Publishing Co.
Copyright 1947, 1956, 1959, 1963 by the University of Nebraska Press
Copyright © 1966 by the Estate of Mari Sandoz
Copyright © 1970 by the Mari Sandoz Corporation
Standard Book Number 8032–0717–4
Library of Congress Catalog Card Number 78–82707
Manufactured in the United States of America

First printing: June 1970
Second printing: August 1970

CONTENTS

INTRODUCTION

The ten selections in this volume were written at intervals from 1929 to 1965, but it would be difficult (without referring to the bibliographical checklist) to say which was the earliest and which the latest. Before her work ever began to appear in national magazines, Mari Sandoz had served a long and gruelling apprenticeship; moreover, she decided early in her career that writers do their best work when they restrict themselves to material with which they have emotional identity. Thus, although these pieces were written over a period of thirty-seven years, they are homogeneous and uniquely Sandoz, not only in style and point of view, but in their characteristic combination of first-hand observation and creative historical vision.

The geographical setting of the first nine of the selections is "Sandoz country"—the Sandhills of northwestern Nebraska—and the people who figure in them are the family and friends and neighbors, redmen and white men, whom the world first came to know in the pages of *Old Jules*. As for the concluding piece, "Outpost in New York," in a sense it may be said to concern "Sandoz country," too, for Mari Sandoz created her own climate wherever she was and she never left the West behind. The selections are arranged according to historical chronology, rather than by date of composition.

When the biography of Mari Sandoz is written, as it surely will be, the biographer will be able to avail himself

of the Mari Sandoz Papers, including many hundreds of
letters, now in the possession of the Sandoz Family Corporation and the University of Nebraska. But the collation
and annotation of these papers is clearly a long-term project, and in planning this collection it was decided that the
content should be limited to previously published work
which the author herself had seen through the press. Five
of the ten selections included were first published by the
University of Nebraska Press, three ("Martha of the
Yellow Braids," "The Neighbor," and "Outpost in New
York") in *Prairie Schooner*, the literary quarterly jointly
sponsored by the University of Nebraska's Department of
English and the UNP, and two ("The Homestead in
Perspective" and "The Christmas of the Phonograph
Records") in Press books. In each instance, of course, the
author reviewed the edited copy before it went to the
printer, and read and okayed galley and page proof. The
other five selections ("The Kinkaider Comes and Goes,"
"Sandhill Sundays," "Musky," "Marlizzie," and "The
Son") were first published elsewhere, but were collected,
re-edited, and published by the UNP in *Hostiles and
Friendlies: Selected Short Writings of Mari Sandoz* (1959).
For that collection, minor cuts were made in "The Kinkaider Comes and Goes," "Musky," "The Son," and
"The Neighbor" to avoid repetition of detail and incident.
The name Jules, Junior, which was used in "The Kinkaider
Comes and Goes" on its first publication, was changed
back to Young Jules, as it had appeared in the original
manuscript, and the title "Marlizzie" was given to the
selection first published as "The New Frontier Woman."
In the case of "The Son," which first appeared in abridged
form as "What the Sioux Taught Me," the original title
and the omitted portions of the text were restored. All
these changes, as well as the copyediting, were discussed
with and accepted by the author, who also checked galley

and page proof. The changes have been retained in the present volume, and the entire text is in the form approved by Mari Sandoz for book publication.

Three of the selections were written prior to the publication of *Old Jules* (1935), which established Miss Sandoz in the front rank of writers on the American West. "The Kinkaider Comes and Goes" was written in 1929 for a course on magazine-article writing given by Professor Sherlock Bronson Gass at the University of Nebraska. It was subtitled "Memories of an adventurous childhood in the Sandhills of Nebraska," and was first published as a two-part piece in the *North American Review* (April, May 1930). "Sandhill Sundays" was written in 1930 and published in *Folksay: A Regional Miscellany* (1931), edited by B. A. Botkin, who had done graduate work at Nebraska with Dr. Louise Pound. "Musky," which develops an episode mentioned in "The Kinkaider Comes and Goes," was written in 1933 and published that same year in *Nature* (November). The other '30's piece, "Marlizzie," which portrays Mari Sandoz' mother, Mary Elizabeth Fehr Sandoz, first appeared as "The New Frontier Woman" in *Country Gentleman* (September 1936).

"Martha of the Yellow Braids" and "The Neighbor" were written in 1945 and appeared in *Prairie Schooner* in, respectively, the issues of Summer 1947 and Winter 1956. "Martha" was subtitled "A Recollection," and in an accompanying note to the late Lowry Charles Wimberly, founder and editor of the *Schooner*, Miss Sandoz wrote: "'Martha' is a piece from my autobiographical files, one of those bits of irrelevant matter that crystallize out of my memory in the heat and pressure of getting a long book together." She sent the companion piece, "The Neighbor," as her contribution to the last issue of the *Schooner* which Professor Wimberly edited before his retirement. Thirty years before he had chosen her story

"The Vine" as the lead piece in the magazine's first issue. "The Son," the single selection dating from the 1950's, first appeared in abridged form in *Empire* (February 24, 1952) and was reprinted in *Reader's Digest* (May 1952). The quotation in italic type preceding "The Son" is taken from an article, "Guerra Ideológica y Militar, Cuatro Novelistas Contemporáneos de Norteamérica," by Thomas Bledsoe in *Cuadernos Americanos* (Mexico), I, January-February, 1952. "The Homestead in Perspective" was a paper presented by Miss Sandoz at the Homestead Centennial Exposition held at the Nebraska Center for Continuing Education, June 11–14, 1962, and was collected in *Land Use Policy and Problems in the United States* (1963), edited by Howard W. Ottoson. "Outpost in New York" was written in 1962 and appeared in *Prairie Schooner* (Summer 1963); it has not previously been collected. "The Christmas of the Phonograph Records" was written in 1965 and was published in book form the following year.

Mari Sandoz expressed herself pungently—and more than once—on the subject of introductions: she thought they should be short. But it will make this one only a few lines longer to end with the words of John K. Hutchens: "Here is a large statement, but, I think, a true one: no one in our time wrote better than the late Mari Sandoz did, or with more authority and grace, about as many aspects of the Old West."

VIRGINIA FAULKNER
Editor
University of Nebraska Press

SANDHILL SUNDAYS
AND OTHER
RECOLLECTIONS

The Homestead in Perspective

The Homestead Act was the hope of the poor man. Many who had wanted a piece of government land felt that pre-empting, which required an eventual cash payment of $1.25 or more an acre, was too risky for the penniless. If the preemptor failed to raise the money at the proper time, in addition to building a home in the wilderness and making a living for a family, he lost the land and with it all his improvements, his work, and his home. The Homestead Act offered any bona fide land seeker 160 acres from the public domain with no cash outlay beyond the $14 filing fee and the improvements he would have to make to live on the place the required five years. His house, barn, sheds and corrals, his well, the tilled acreage and the fencing, all counted toward the final patent to the land, and most of these improvements could be made by the homesteader's own hands, his and the family's.

It was this offer of free land that drew my father, Old Jules Sandoz, west to a homestead in the unorganized region that was to become Sheridan County, Nebraska, and he stressed "free land" in all the letters he wrote to the European and American newspapers for the working man, letters that drew the hundreds of settlers he located.

3

The home seeker, as late as the end of the Kinkaid Homestead days of my childhood, came by every possible means, even afoot. I was born too late to see the Czechoslovakian couple who crossed much of Nebraska pushing a wheelbarrow loaded with all their belongings, including, it was said, the wedding feather tick. But we saw many land seekers walk in, some coming much farther than the seventeen miles from the railroad. There were dusty men, worn and discouraged until they got a good wash-up at the Niobrara River near our house or at our well, followed by one of Mother's hearty suppers and a big dose of Old Jules' enthusiasm and faith in the country. Some came by livery rig or the mail wagon, or were picked up by a settler returning home from town. Many of the more serious land seekers left their families back east until they were located. Often these drove in by wagon in the old way although the wire fences of settlers, and, in the free-land regions, the cattlemen, prevented the accustomed movement up along the streams, as Old Jules himself had come, following the Niobrara to Mirage Flats.

We children had the usual curiosity about outsiders but we were even more thoroughly disciplined than most homesteader children, who were taught to keep out of the way and never push into grown-up affairs. But we tried to hear the answer to Old Jules usual western query: "What name you traveling under?"

This question from a rough, bearded man with a strong foreign accent and a gun on his arm was not reassuring to strangers. But perhaps a potential settler should realize from the start that homesteading was not for the timid, and as soon as a man could say "I'm looking for me a piece of government land—" he was among friends. He and any family he had were welcome to eat at our table and sleep in our beds even if we children were moved to the floor. This was naturally all free beyond the twenty-five

dollar locating and surveying fee Old Jules charged whenever the settler managed to get the money. Often the
family stayed with us until their house was up, the wife
perhaps criticizing Father's profane and bawdy tongue
and complaining contemptuously about Mother's bread
from unbleached macaroni wheat that we grew and hauled
to the water mill on Pine Creek.

For us children the important home seekers were the
boomers, the covered wagon families. Evenings we
watched them come down into the Niobrara valley,
rumble over the plank bridge, and climb the steep sandy
pitch to the bench on which our house stood. There, on a
flat camping-ground, the panting horses were allowed to
stop, and barefoot children spilled out of the wagon, front
and back, to run, galloping and bucking like calves let out
of a pen. We stared from among the cherry trees, or in the
summer, from the asparagus patch where the greenery
stood over our heads. We saw the tugs dropped, the harness stripped off and piled against the wagon tongue, while
the woman ordered the children to this and that task as the
fire began to smoke in the little pile of stones always there
for campers.

Finally the man might come to draw a bucket of the
clear water from our well, water so cold it hurt the teeth
on hot days.

By the time we were old enough to notice, Father had
no trouble waiting until after supper to talk land to such
men.

"Boomers!" he would say, in contempt. "Probably
been to Oregon and back, living off the country, picking
up anything that's loose. Hey, Mari, go hide all the ham-
mers and bring in my rifle—" meaning the 30-30 that
usually hung on the antlers outside the door.

"And shut up the chickens—" Mother would add.

Old Jules was usually right about the boomers of the 1906–12 period. The man would come in to talk land but even if he showed any enthusiasm for homesteading, the family might be pulling out at dawn, seldom with anything of consequence that belonged to us. That stack of guns in a corner of our kitchen–living room, and Father's evident facility with firearms, discouraged more than petty thefts of, say, a pair of pliers or a slab of bacon from the smokehouse.

"Sneaky thieves!" Mother would snort. "If they were so hungry I would have given them more than that, so long as we could spare it."

A few stayed to follow Father's buckskin team into the sandhills, to live in the covered wagon until a dugout or a soddy could be prepared on the new homestead. Some of these left when the drouth and hot winds of August struck, along with others who had walked in or came by hired rig. The winters seemed particularly hard to the latter-day boomers, and often the first fall blizzard sent them rolling toward Texas or Arkansas. Some stuck it out. Several of these Kinkaid-day boomers are growing fine blooded stock in Nebraska, the older members spending the winters in Florida or California and damning the government.

We tend to forget that the homesteaders were not a type, not as alike as biscuits cut out with a baking-powder can. They varied as much as their origins and their reasons for coming west. There were Daughters and Sons of the Revolution located next to the communal communities of the Mennonites, say, or the Hutterians. An illiterate from some other frontier might be neighboring with a Greek and Hebrew scholar from a colony of Russian Jews in the Dakotas. A nervous-fingered murderer who fled west under a new name might join fences with a non-violent River Baptist or a vegetarian who wouldn't kill a rabbit eating up his first sprouts of lettuce, no matter how hungry the settler might be.

Yet there was apparently a certain repetition of characters in the homestead communities. Those who thought that Old Jules Sandoz was incredible or at least unique should go through the many thousands of letters I received from homesteaders and descendants of homesteaders. Apparently, men with some Old Julesian traits lived in every pioneer community—even as far away as Australia and New Zealand—men with the vision of the community builder, the stubbornness to stick against every defeat, the grim ruthlessness required to hold both themselves and their neighbors to the unwelcoming virgin land.

There was considerable difference between the homesteaders who came into western Nebraska in the 1884–90 period and the Kinkaiders of 1906–12, that is, after the cattleman fences were removed from the government land. The homesteaders of the earlier period were generally young, many under the required twenty-one years, but with a family or a flexible conscience. In the height of the Kinkaid Homestead days many were in their forties and some much older—usually office workers or teachers and so on—retired people or those who had lost their jobs in the retrenchment of 1906–08. There were many women among these, not only among the fraudulent entries by the cattlemen (often only names of old-soldier widows) but among the bona fide homesteaders. These women were classified roughly into two groups by the other settlers. Those with genteel ways, graying hair, downy faces and perhaps good books to loan to a settler's reading-hungry daughter, were called Boston school teachers, no matter who or where from. The others, called Chicago widows, weren't young either, or pretty, but their talk, their dress, and their ways were gayer, more colorful, more careless; their books, if any, were paperback novels, with such titles as *Wife in Name Only,* or *Up from the Depths.* Several had a volume of nonfiction called *From Ballroom to Hell,* with every step of the way well illustrated and described. Among the tips offered was a solution for a recurring problem: To fill out your corset cover, roll up two stockings and pin into place, but be sure the stockings are clean, to avoid an offending odor.

It is true that in the largely male population of our homestead regions more of the Chicago widows got married than the Boston school ma'am type.

There was a saying among the settlers that the first spring of a new homesteader told whether the man or the woman was the boss. If the house was put up first, plainly the woman ran things; if a corn patch was broken out before any building, the cowboys told each other that this homesteader would be hard to drive off. But there were other factors to be considered. An April settler was wise to throw up a claim shack of some kind and leave the sod breaking for May, after the grass was started well enough so it would be killed by the plowing. Nor were the women, bossy or not, always easy to drive out. Some clung to the homestead even after their husbands were shot down by ranch hirelings. Nebraska's State Senator Cole grew up in the sandhills because his mother stayed with her two young sons after their father was shot off his mower.

Old Jules' first claim dwelling was half dugout, half sod, but the home of his family was a frame house in which the water froze in the teakettle in January. We envied our neighbors with good sod houses, the deep window seats full of Christmas cactus, century plants, and geraniums blooming all winter, the fine shadowiness of the interior cool and grateful in the summer, while our house was hot as an iron bucket in the sun. Old Jules permitted no cooling blinds or curtains at the windows. He wanted to see anyone coming up. Evenings he always sat back out of line of the lighted windows.

Although I never lived in a sod house I went to school in one and taught school in two others, both pretty decrepit at the time, with mouse holes in the walls; one with a friendly bullsnake living there. Sometimes the snake was fooled by the glowing stove on a chilly fall day and came wandering out and down the aisle during school hours. A snickering among the boys always warned me, and the snake too. Licking out his black forked tongue speculatively, the autumn-logy snake turned slowly around and moved back to his hole in the wall.

The three immediate needs of the new settler were shelter, food, and water. Of the three, only the food that he must grow had a tyrannical season. As locator Old Jules never showed a home seeker a place without a piece of corn land. At a potential site he would push his hat back, estimate the arable acreage, and sink his spade into an average spot. Turning up a long sod, he examined the depth and the darkness of the top soil and shook out the rooting of the grass. If he was satisfied, he looked around at the weeds, not just on spots enriched by some animal carcass long ago, but in general. Where sunflowers grew strong and tall, corn would do well.

But even the best of sod had to be turned and planted at the proper time. With two fairly good draft horses, preferably three or four against the tough rooting, and a sod plow, the settler could break the prairie himself. Or he could hire it done, usually by exchange of work with some of his neighbors. I like to remember the look on the faces of some of these new homesteaders as they tilled the first bit of earth they ever owned. Like any toddler, when I was two, three years old I couldn't be kept from following in the furrow of any plowing done near the house. Later it

seemed to me there was something like a spiritual excitement about a man guiding a breaker bottom through
virgin earth, with the snap and crackle of the tough roots
as they were cut, the sod rolling smooth and flat from the
plow, a gull or two following for the worms, and black-
birds chattering around.

Sometimes corn, beans, or potatoes were dropped in the
furrow behind the sod plow and covered by the next
round but more often the corn was planted later by a man,
a woman, or an energetic boy or girl. With an apron or a
bag tied on for the seed, and a spade in the hand, the planter
started. At every full man's step, or two steps for the
shorter-legged, the spade was thrust down into the sod,
worked sideways to widen the slit, two kernels of corn
dropped in, the spade swung out and the foot brought
down on the cut to seal it. All day, up and down the sod
ribbons, the rythmic swing of step and thrust was main-
tained. To be sure, the spade arm was mighty work-sore
the next morning, but every homesteader's child learned
that the remedy for that was more work.

Millions of acres were planted this way, sometimes with
beans and pumpkin seeds mixed with the corn for a stretch.
Good breaking grew few weeds except a scattering of big
sunflowers, so the sod field was little care. With the luck
of an early August rain, turnip and rutabaga seed could be
broadcast between a stretch of rows for the winter root pit.
Up in South Dakota, some homesteaders tried flax instead
of corn, the seed harrowed into the sod just before a rain,
and were rewarded by an expanse as blue as fallen sky in
blooming time.

The second spring the sod was backset, and ready for
small grain, perhaps oats or rye but more often the newer
varieties of wheat broadcast on the fresh plowing from a
bag slung under one arm, much like the figure of the
Sower on the Nebraska capitol. The seed was covered by

a harrow or drag. If there was no harrow, a heavily branched tree, a hackberry, perhaps, would be dragged over the ground by the old mares or patient oxen. Mechanical seeders drawn by fast-paced horses or mules helped spread bonanza wheat farming from the Red River down to Oklahoma and deep into Montana and Alberta. But the new homesteader still broadcast his small grain by hand.

The settler too late for the land along the streams was in urgent need of water from the day of his arrival. True, there might be buffalo wallows and other ponds filled by the spring rains for the stock a while, but many settlers hauled at least the household water ten, twelve miles, and farther, until a well could be put down, or had to be, to quiet the womenfolks. Where the water table was not too deep the first well was usually dug—cheap but dangerous for the novice. Every community had its accidents and tragedies. Uncurbed wells caved in on the digger. People, adults and children, fell into the uncovered holes and were perhaps rescued by a desperate effort of everyone within fifty miles around, or were left buried there, with a flower or a tree planted to mark the grave.

The well in our home yard was the usual dug one, curbed to the bottom, with a windlass and a bucket that had been a black powder can, larger than the usual pail, the fifty-pound powder size, I think, and came painted a waterproof blue outside. All of us were very careful around wells, perhaps because we had a constant example before us. Old Jules was crippled his first summer on his claim on Mirage Flats. He had finished his new well and was being drawn up by his helpers. As he neared the top the two practical jokers yanked the rope to scare him. The rope, frayed by all the strain of lifting the soil from the sixty-five foot hole, broke. The digger was dropped to the bottom and crippled for the rest of his life. Only the extraordinary luck of getting to Dr. Walter Reed, of later yellow-fever fame, at the frontier post, Fort Robinson, kept him alive at all.

Our well on the river had a solid ladder inside the casing, the kind of ladder that could have saved Old Jules all those crippled years if he had nailed one into the curbing of his first well and climbed out instead of standing in the dirt bucket to be drawn up. Whenever a foolish hen jumped up on the water bench of our well and let the wind blow her in, it was Old Jules who clambered ponderously down the deep hole after her. Practically any other emergency, except something like sewing up a badly cut leg, he let his wife or his children handle—ordered them to handle—but he was determined there would not be another well accident in his household.

In the deep-soiled sand hills, most homesteaders put down their wells with a sand bucket—a valve-tipped short piece of pipe on a rope to be jerked up and down inside the larger well piping that had an open sand point at the bottom. Water was poured into the pipe, to turn the soil into mud under the plunging sand bucket and be picked up by the valve in the end. Full, it was drawn out, emptied and the process repeated. Occasionally, the larger pipe was given a twist with a wrench until its own weight forced it down as fast as the earth below was soaked and lifted out in the sand bucket. When a good water table was reached the end of the sand point was plugged, a cylinder and pumprod put in, and attached to a pump, homemade or bought from a mail order catalogue, and the homesteader had water.

"Nothing's prettier'n a girl pumpin' water in the wind," the cowboys used to say, obviously of homesteader daughters, for no others were out pumping.

As long as there were buffaloes, settlers could go out to the herd ranges for meat and even a few hides to sell for that scarcest of pioneer commodities, cash in the palm. The early settlers learned to preserve a summer buffalo or two in the Indian way, cutting the meat into flakes thin as the edge of a woman's hand to dry quickly in the hot winds, with all the juices preserved. Well-dried, the meat kept for months and was good boiled with a touch of prairie onion or garlic. With vegetables, the dried buffalo or deer or elk made good boiled dinners or meat pies, and was chopped into cornmeal mush by the Pennsylvanians for scrapple until there was pork.

Much could be gleaned for the table before the garden even started. Old Jules brought water cress seed west and scattered it wherever there was a swift current and in the lake regions where the earth-warmed water seeped out all winter, and kept an open spot for cress and mallard ducks. Dandelions start early and as soon as they came up brownish red, we cut them out with a knife for salad, very good with hard boiled eggs, the dressing made with vinegar from wild currants, plums, or grapes and the vinegar-mother we borrowed from a neighbor who had brought it in a bottle by wagon from Kentucky. Later there was lambsquarter, boiled and creamed and perhaps on baking days spread into a *dunna*, which looked like a green-topped pizza. Meat the homesteaders could provide—antelope and deer, and after these were gone, grouse, quail, and cottontails, with ducks and geese spring and fall. Old Jules was an excellent trapper and hunter as well as gardener and horticulturist, with his wife and the children for the weeding and the harvest. Consequently we seldom lacked anything in food except the two items that cost money—sugar and coffee. Roasted rye made a cheap and poor coffee substitute. Other homesteaders grew cane and cooked the sap into hard and soft sorghum but our sweetening was often nothing but dried fruits eaten from the palm or baked into buns and rolls. Once a whole winter was sweetened by a barrel of extra dark blackstrap molasses Father got somehow as a bargain. It made fine pungent cookies.

Mother was a good pig raiser and we usually had wonderful sausage looped over broomsticks in the smoke house with the hams and bacon, the good sweet lard in the cellar in crocks. In our younger days butchering was a trial. It meant Father had to be disturbed from his plans, his thinking, to shoot the fat hog. The washboiler was put on the stove, with buckets and the teakettle filled with extra scalding water. A barrel had to be set tilted into the ground with an old door laid on low blocks up against the open barrelhead. When everything was ready, the hog up close and everybody out to keep it there, Old Jules had to be called, Mother shouting to him, "That one there! Shoot quick!"

But by then the hog might be gone, to be fetched back after a chase through the trees. When Father got a shot he put the bullet cleanly between the eyes but he was often experimenting with the amount of powder that would kill without penetrating into the good meat. Sometimes the hog was not even stunned but ran squealing for the brush, and had to be shot again. Sometimes it fell soundlessly and Mother thrust the sticking knife into Father's hand. With disgust all over his face, he drove the knife in the general direction of the jugular vein and when the dark blood welled out, stepped back while Mother ran in to roll the animal to make the blood flow faster. When Grandmother was still alive she usually hurried out with a pan for the makings of her blood pudding but none of the rest of the family would even taste it.

Now the hog was dragged up on the old door, ready

for the scalding. Everybody ran for the boiling water, the washboiler, the buckets.

"Look out! Look out!" Father kept shouting most of the time as he limped around. When the barrel was steaming with the hot water, he and Mother shoved the dead pig down into it head first, because that was the hardest to scald well, and worked the carcass back and forth by the hind feet, to get every spot wet, while Mother yanked off handsful of the loosening bristles, shaking the heat from her fingers. Then the hog was drawn out upon the door, turned and the hind half thrust into the stinking hot water, and pulled out upon the door again. Now everybody fell to scraping, clutching butcher knives by the back or working with ragged-edge tin cans, the bristles rolling off in wet clumps and windrows.

No butchered animal looks finer than a well-scalded and scraped hog—pink and plump and appetizing. That evening there was fresh liver for supper, and the frothing brain cooked in a frying pan. I liked pork tenderloin with the animal heat and sweetness still in it. I fried this for myself, and never tasted a finer dish. Meat still animal-warm was credited with helping to cure many sufferers from bleeding stomachs sent west to a government claim by their doctors. Whole communities of stomach patients settled on the Plains, and usually died of other complaints, including old age.

Butchering for most homesteaders, particularly the lone ones, was a matter for neighborly help, as were many larger undertakings, particularly threshing. Most of the threshing outfits that finally reached the homesteader were small horse-powered machines with the owner probably feeding the separator himself to keep greenhorns from choking it, tearing it up. Usually three, four hands, including the horse-power driver, came with the outfit. The rest of the sixteen, eighteen man crew was drawn from the settlers, exchanging work. Often neighbor women came to help with the cooking. Reputations were made or broken by the meals put out for the threshers, and many a plain daughter owed a good marriage match to the wild plum pie or the chicken and dumplings of her mother at thresh-ing time.

   The homesteader got most of his outside items through mail order catalogues, including, sometimes, his wife, if one could call the matrimonial papers, the heart-and-hand publications, catalogues. They did describe the offerings rather fully but with, perhaps, a little less honesty than Montgomery Ward or Sears Roebuck. Unmarried wom-en were always scarce in new regions. Many bachelor settlers had a sweetheart back east or in the Old Country, or someone who began to look a little like a sweetheart from the distance of a government claim that got more and more lonesome as the holes in the socks got bigger. Some of these girls never came. Others found themselves in an unexpectedly good bargaining position and began to make all kinds of demands in that period of feminine uprising. They wanted the husband to promise abstinence from profanity, liquor, and tobacco and perhaps even commanded allegiance to the rising cause of woman suffrage. Giving up the cud of tobacco in the cheek was often very difficult. A desperate neighbor of ours chewed grass, bitter willow and cottonwood leaves, coffee grounds, and finally sent away for a tobacco cure. It made him sick, so sick, at least in appearance, that his new wife begged him to take up chewing again. Others back-slid on the sly, sneaking a chew of Battle Axe or Horseshoe in the face of certain anger and tears.
   But many bachelors had no sweetheart to come out, and some of these started to carry the heart-and-hand papers around until the pictures of the possible brides were worn

off the page. In those days the usual purpose really was marriage, not luring the lonely out of their pitiful little savings or even their lives. " We married everything that got off the railroad," old homesteaders, including my father, used to say.

Usually the settler was expected to send the prospective wife a stagecoach or railroad ticket. Perhaps, even though he had mortgaged his team to get the ticket, the woman sold it and never came and there was nothing to be done unless the U.S. mails were involved. Most of the women did arrive and many of these unions, bound by mutual need and dependence, founded excellent families. Of course, there was no way to compel a mail order wife to stay when she saw the husband's place. Usually she had grown up in a settled region, perhaps with Victorian sheltering, and was shocked by her new home, isolated, at the best a frame or log shack with cracks for the blizzard winds, or only a soddy or dugout into some bank, with a dirt floor and the possibility of wandering stock falling through the roof.

The long distance to the stagecoach or the railroad, with walking not good, kept many a woman to her bargain. There are, however, stories of desperate measures used to hold the wife—ropes or chains or locked leg hobbles, but the more common and efficacious expedient was early pregnancy. That brought the customary gift for the first child—a sewing machine, and many a man, including my own father, scratched mightily for the money.

The women, particularly the young ones, brought some gaiety to the homestead regions, with visitings, berryings, pie socials, square dances, play parties, literaries at the schools, and shivarees for the newlyweds. The women organized Sunday schools, and sewing bees. When calamity or sickness struck, the women went to help, and if there was death they bathed and dressed the corpse, coming with dishes of this and that so the bereaved need not trouble to cook and were spared the easing routine. Doctors were usually far away and scarce and expensive. Old Jules, with his partial training in medicine, had a shelf of the usual remedies and for years he was called out to care for the difficult deliveries. Several times middle-aged people have come to me to say that Old Jules brought them into the world, perhaps back in the 1880's or 1890's.

There were problems besides sickness and death, besides the lack of cash and credit that dogs every new community, besides the isolation and drouth and dust storms. Fires swept over the prairies any time during practically ten months a year, although the worst were usually in the fall, with the grass standing high and rich in oily seed. The prairie fires could be set by fall lightning, by the carelessness of greenhorns in the country, by sparks from the railroads, and by deliberate malice.

"Burning a man out" could mean destroying his grass, crops, hay, even his house and himself. Once started, the heat of the fire created a high wind that could sweep it over a hundred miles of prairie in an incredibly short time. Settlers soon learned to watch the horizon for the pearling rise of smoke from prairie grass. At the first sign of this, everyone hurried to fight the flames with water barrels, gunny sacks, hoes, and particularly plows to turn furrows for the backfiring. Even more important was the awareness of the danger ahead of time, early enough so fireguards were plowed around the homestead, at least around the buildings. In addition everyone was told the old Indian advice: "Come fire, go for bare ground, sand or gravel or to big water. Make a backfire against small creek or bare spot, to burn only into wind, and stay where ashes are. Best is to go on a place with no grass, and do not run."

Old Jules' Kinkaid in the sandhills bordered on the Osborne Valley, which had a prairie-fire story. An earlier settler and his wife and two small boys had lived in the Osborne—a wet hay flat with miles of rushes and dense canebrakes, and a small open lake in the center that dried up in the summers. Early one fall a prairie fire came sweeping in toward the place. The settler and his wife hurried out to help fight the flames, commanding the two boys to stay in the house. It was sod, with a sod roof, and surrounded by a wide fireguard. Here they were safe. But when the smoke thickened and the fire came roaring over the hill toward the house the boys ran in terror to the swamp, clambering through the great piles of dead rushes and canes for the lake bed. The fire caught them.

After that the settler and his wife moved away but the story of the boys remained as a warning to all of us. When my brother James and I were sent down to hold the Kinkaid for a few months alone, we often went to the Osborne swamp to hunt ducks but never without searching the horizon for prairie-fire smoke. There were mushrooms growing where the sod house of the early settler had been, good mushrooms, fine fried with young ducks or prairie chicken.

The most dreaded storm of the upper homestead region was and still is the blizzard. The first one to kill many people was the Buffalo Hunter's Storm of the 1870's, although the School Children's Blizzard of 1888 is sadly remembered, and even the one of 1949. Most of the people who died in blizzards died through some foolishness, some stupidity, and a few years later would have known better. There are always signs before the worst storms: unseasonal warmth, calm, and stillness, as on January 12, 1888, and old timers were ready with warnings of what to do if caught in a blizzard. "If lost in the sand hills, any blowout will give the directions. The wind cuts the hollows from the northwest and moves the sand out southeastward. If so confused that directions are useless or you are too far from shelter, dig in anywhere to keep dry, with a fire if possible, but dry, even if it's only under a bank somewhere, into the dry sand of a blowout. Don't get yourself wet and *don't* wear yourself out. Practically anyone with a little sense and a little luck can outlast a blizzard."

Not all the danger is in the storm itself. The homestead region had few trees and fewer rocks and a May blizzard left an unbelievable glare of unbroken whiteness in the high spring sun, enough to make cows snowblind, and people, if the eyes were not protected. Of all the dangers of homestead life, our family escaped all but two, Old Jules' well accident and my snowblindness in a May blizzard that cost me all useful sight in one eye.

Much of what I have been saying comes out of my childhood but could have come out of the childhood of practically anyone brought up on a homestead. Those first years on a government claim were a trial, a hardship for the parents, particularly the women, but the men too. Usually only one in four entrymen remained to patent the claim; in the more difficult regions and times only one in ten, or even fifteen. A large percentage of those into any new region had been misfits in their home community, economic, social, or emotional misfits, both the men and the women. Some of these, unsettled by the hardships and the isolation, ended in institutions or suicide if they did not drift on or flee back to relatives or in-laws. Those who stayed might be faced by drouth, grasshoppers, and ten-cent corn, sometimes followed by the banker's top buggy come to attach the mortgaged team or the children's milk cow. The men gathered at the sales and at political meetings, with many women, too, speaking for reforms, for a better shake for the sparsely settled, sparsely represented regions.

None of these things could be kept from the children. They saw the gambles of life and the size of the stakes. They shared in the privation and the hard work. All of us knew children who put in twelve-, fourteen-hour days from March to November. We knew seven-, eight-year-old boys who drove four-horse teams to the harrow, who shocked grain behind the binder all day in heat and dust and rattlesnakes, who cultivated, hoed and weeded corn, and finally husked it out before they could go to school in November. And even then there were the chores morning and evening, the stock to feed, the cows to milk by lantern light. If there had been tests for muscular fitness as compared to European children then, we would have held our own.

Often there was no difference in the work done by the boys and the girls, except that the eldest daughter of a sizable family was often a serious little mother by the time she was six, perhaps baking up a 49-pound sack of flour every week by the time she was ten. Such children learned about life before they had built up any illusions and romanticisms to be clung to later, at the expense of maturity. Almost from their first steps, the homesteader's children had to meet new situations, make decisions, develop a self-discipline if they were to survive. They learned dependence upon one's neighbors, and discovered the interrelationships of earth and sky and animal and man. They could see, in their simpler society, how national and international events conditioned every day of their existence. They learned to rescue themselves in adulthood as they had once scrabbled under the fence when the heel flies drove the milk cows crazy. What they didn't have they tried to make for themselves, earned money to buy, or did without. Perhaps somewhere there are individuals from homestead childhoods who grab for fellowships and grants, for scholarships and awards, for special influence and privilege but I don't know of any. The self-reliance, often the fierce independence, of a homestead upbringing seems to stay with them. They may wander far from their roots, for they are children of the uprooted, but somehow their hearts are still back there with the old government claim.

The Kinkaider Comes and Goes

On a gatepost twenty-five miles over the wind-swept hills from the nearest railroad hangs a tipsy sign. Many winter snows, many summer suns, have weathered it, mellowed it to a velvety gray. Precariously creaking on one nail, the first storm will cast it down, unlamented, into the jointed sandgrass.

While the boiling engine of the mail truck cooled from the long pull through the sandy gap, I shook the wrinkles from my skirt and idly inspected the blurred legend: "Pleasant Home." No pleasantness here to sun-blinded eyes. Only a little valley carpeted with russet bunchgrass tucked in between towering hills whose highest dunes are bald among clusters of green-black yuccas. Decidedly no home.

But in a clump of ragged sunflowers stood an old cook-stove, the corroded oven door sagging to reveal hay and straw of a mouse nest where spicy cookies once baked. And suddenly it all came back; the little white beehive of a house with a green blind at the one window—the home of a spinster music teacher from Chicago and one of the first of a dozen of these "music boxes" as the cowboys dubbed them. A rare pleasantness, too, crept over me: the soft haze of a heat-dance on the far gap; brown shading to cream yellow on the hill slopes; the whitish horizon, streaked with wind, blending to deepest blue overhead. Memories relegated to mental attics by years at college and at work revived in my consciousness. This patch of sand-hills stretching from the Niobrara River to the Platte was the Jötunheim of my childhood, spent upon its fringes. Out of this almost mythical land, apparently so monotonous, so passionless, came wondrous and fearful tales of gray wolves that leaped upon fat yearlings (probably because of the scarcity of children)—and of rattlesnakes—and of cattlemen.

That the grays existed, my brothers and I knew. Once, when reports of unusual ravages reached our father, Jules Sandoz, pioneer locator and trapper, he set out on a hunting trip with Jim, a convict on parole to him. The diminutive buckskin team, through their fondness for spectacular runaways, pulled an odd wagon out of our yard that midwinter morning. Piled high with equipment covered by a huge calico feather tick roped down, it looked much like a fat blue sausage on wheels.

Two weeks later the unwashed men came back, half-frozen, but jubilant. They had poisoned one of the largest grays ever taken in Nebraska; a difficult feat, for the gray wolf eats only his own kill. Fortunately, they found a half-eaten rabbit on the animal's trail. A large dose of strychnine did the rest. The pelt brought $110, mostly cattlemen bounty, altogether a magnificent sum. But much to Mother's consternation, the money went for more guns, traps, and ammunition.

Such evidence of vulnerability reduced our respect for wolf stories related before the wood-filled heater on winter nights. The cattlemen, however, remained fabulous beings, something like the capitalists pictured in the *Appeal to Reason*, our household paper in those days, only their bellicosity was the result of gorging on public lands, a sacred something that existed, apparently, only in the sand-hills. Specifically, we knew a boy, not much older than our own pre-school years, whose father was said to have been shot from his own windmill by a hired killer. And the rifle the boy's mother drew upon the murderer had proved empty! That catastrophe, my brother Young Jules and I consoled ourselves, could not happen in our home. The Sandoz arsenal was always loaded to the muzzle, or, rather, muzzles; and Father had been a crack shot since the early eighties, when he roamed the hills with the Indians.

The thin crust of security we thus built over our exist-ence was rudely and finally broken by a horseman who rode wildly into our yard, his rifle balanced across his saddle. He had fenced a little Government land near a large ranch, and that morning he found an old whisky bottle on his doorstep. In it was a rifle shell wrapped in an unsigned note telling him to get out or be carried out.

The smell of hot lead stung our nostrils that night as Father molded bullets and we children dipped the shiny slugs in melted beeswax and set them in rows like marching soldiers to cool. It was good fun, and not until one of the few indulgences Jules Sandoz permitted his family, and one valued accordingly, was forgotten did we sense the gravity of the occasion. That night there was no burning of a pinch of smokeless powder in Father's palm, accom-panied by his usual explanation that the force of this explo-sive depended upon confinement. Instead we were marched off to bed early.

Through my crack in the wall I watched Father limp about on his stiff ankle, a reminder of his first dug well and the subsequent long months in the hospital at Fort Robinson. Now he took down one gun after another, ejecting the factory-loaded shells with steel-jacketed or soft-nosed bullets. Reloaded ammunition was used for target practice only.

Calculatingly, he rolled the heavy shells in his palm, his sharp eyes confident upon those of the nervous little man beside him. The two guns over his bed, a thirty-thirty and a twelve-gauge pump-gun "for close range," the forty-five–seventy over the lounge in the kitchen–living room, the thirty-thirty outside the door on the bleached deer antlers—all were examined; even the little group behind the door. Mother sat close to the lamp, bending over her glinting needle, mending socks. Once or twice she looked up, her mouth a thin line, but she dropped her head without speaking.

The next morning there was a great deal of target shooting. Father sent spurts of sand from the exact center of a yellowish spot, little larger than a tablecloth, on a hillside across the Niobrara. Encouraged to loquacity, the frightened man of yesterday talked endlessly about "boring him full of daylight," meaning, we knew, the rancher suspected of sending the note. And finally the two men vanished into the hills together. A week later Father came back. The man stayed, unmolested.

Upon that prelude, the tempo of our life accelerated. Mysterious men, Government agents, Mother called them, came out in shiny top buggies. They carried rolls of semi-transparent, bluish maps, and after supper, with Father, they pored over them for hours, talking a meaningless jargon of figures, corners, correction lines, old soldiers' claims, and fictitious filings. Over the shoulder of a less formidable one we caught glimpses of these plats, ruled into squares through which ran funny black marks, indicating, the man told me, ridges of hills. Obliterated and faked corners, buried plow shares and sickle bars to detract the compass needle, and final delvings into Father's deer hunting days in the eighties, when the corners were new, lengthened the evenings.

Early in the morning the men usually started into the hills, the Government man driving, while Father watched the roadside for a grouse or a rabbit, his pump gun between his knees, the barrel against his shoulder, brushing his unkempt beard. Now and then he pushed the old cap, either of muskrat or of equally shapeless cloth, back from his eyes as he scanned the horizon. The thirty-thirty rifle was always across the buggy bed at his feet.

Rapidly one exciting event followed another: Government indictment of the larger cattle outfits for fictitious filings and fraudulent fencing of public lands; troops that cut the barbed wire fences when the cattlemen refused to tear them down; Father gone to Omaha as a Government witness; his picture in the daily papers, his rifle still across his forearm.

Strange men came and went, men we were forbidden to mention to our rare playmates. Always curious, I discovered that one of these wore a revolver in his armpit and had a shiny button, like a star, that he kept hidden. "Nosey brat!" he called me when I asked him why he didn't carry his gun like the cowboys that stopped to water the dusty, gaunt herds of cattle they were stringing into the hills. Once or twice furtive ranch owners called, ostensibly to look over the few Indian ponies we had for sale.

"We'll see you're taken care of, Jule," I overheard one of them promise, flipping the end of a packet of bills.

But Father was stubborn in his contention that he wanted to build up the country. The result was that several of the indictments led to convictions. A couple of cattle kings went to prison. The fraudulent filings that covered every desirable section were canceled and the sandhills were now actually opened for settlement. Through the sudden effectiveness of the abused Kinkaid Act, some

mysterious person in Washington, surely a god! was dol-
ing out the land within these soapweed marred slopes in
640 acre chunks to any apparently bona fide homeseeker.

And now came our first covered wagon. True, there had
been others, dimly remembered, but this was tangible
reality as it swayed drunkenly down the hill, rumbled over
the plank bridge, and climbed the rise, drawn by two slow
horses, followed by two colts and a lazy yellow cow with
her calf tied to her tail. Amid loud shoutings from the
black-bearded driver and nickerings from the horses, the
wagon stopped on the little level spot across the road from
our house. Many children tumbled out, leaping and playing in their release. What fine playfellows they were, and
how interesting the wagon was, stacked up and dark, much
like our attic.

That wagon was the vanguard of a long line of homeseekers that passed through our little world. Strange
people, these, from far-away places, the men always seek-
ing Paradise over the next hill, the women gaunt and silent
or scolding in high, nervous voices. Impatiently they
waited for Father or started out alone.

To take such people into the hills, run a line from a
known corner to a desirable location, and then take them
to the land office at Alliance to file or contest was the business of Jules Sandoz. For this service, requiring a week or
ten days, he received $25. Usually the settler had only a
portion of that sum or none of it, so he got his home "on
tick" or "on pump," meaning, in sandhill parlance, he
charged it. Most of the settlers paid eventually, often in
rye or corn they grew from seed that also came "on tick"
from the locator.

And every so often a well-meaning meddler would
warn Mother that sooner or later, when the Government
vigilance was lowered, the cattlemen would strike. Many
homeseekers, too, were discouraged by tales of starvation

spread by ranchers or were frightened by the stories of this
or that settler who was hauled out of the hills by his widow
after a sad "accident." But nothing really alarming had
happened—probably nothing would.

Then, July 2, 1908, a young school teacher, new in the
community, tore madly into our yard. His face was paper
white and his day-old beard was like a black smudge along
his chin. Mother ran to meet him, her hands under her
apron, her face anxious.

"Emile's been shot!" he shouted.

Mother's hands dropped heavily to her sides.

"How?"

"While he was branding his calves in the corral, before
the whole family.* Ralph Nieman, the damned skunk,
rode up, shot him in the back, and then rode away!"

Weakly, Mother dropped to the woodblock in the front
yard. So it had come! Father's brother, who never located
a settler, who was, in fact, rather friendly to the small
cattlemen about him. He lived only five miles away, on
Pine Creek, with his wife and seven children.

And Father was locating in the hills, had been gone for
three days!

All evening our barbed-wire telephone line was busy.
The sheriff had been down; had the murderer. He didn't
have him; he hadn't even gone out. The man had shot
himself; no, he had shot someone else. By the next noon
the situation was clarified. The sheriff had not sought the
murderer until the next morning. Community feeling ran
high; the young teacher talked of mobbing, of searching
the upper ranch, located in a wet hay flat full of willows.
Without able leadership the plan collapsed. They waited
for Father, who had once been the leader of a vigilante-like
group. But he was in the hills, in that land of endless dun-
colored hills where chops and blowouts follow each other

---

* Later reports: he was milking a cow, the boys holding the calf off.

like waves of a wind-whipped sea. Across the road camped two groups of homeseekers, apparently not understanding the situation.

A day passed. Uncle Emile was still alive with a bullet in his lungs. Two days—three. Uncle Emile was dead. The settlers' wagons creaked away across the river. And still there were no signs of Father. A reward was offered for the murderer, who, some said, was surely across the border, north or south, by now. Or perhaps in the deeper hills. Maybe he would sneak up to a hilltop as hunters once did for deer and antelope, bareheaded, looking from behind a soapweed, only it would be a man he was stalking, a man in the valley, sighting through his compass, his back to the killer.

And then Father came home.

With my baby sister astride my hip I ran to tell him. He knew. Above the dark beard his face, commonly so ruddy from wind and sun, was greenish yellow. I dropped behind my mother, afraid.

The funeral was that afternoon.

"You ought to go," Mother reasoned. "What will people say?"

But Father didn't go. He lay on the couch under the window, watching the neighbors drive past, his rifle within reach. On their way back, several of them stopped, wondering, generally considering Father's caution wise. An associate of the murderer's, not debonair, handsome, as the killer, but stocky and red-faced, with whitish pig eyes, stood at the outskirts of the crowd a while; and then rode away. It was whispered that he was looking for the locator, also that Uncle Emile was killed because he gossiped, knew too much and told too much about the ranchers. I ran into the garden. Was there anything about them that Father didn't know?

That evening, while Mother was doing the chores and

Father inspected the orchard, using his rifle as a cane, I nailed the three windows in their bedroom down with ten-penny nails. The house door had no lock, but I drove a spike diagonally into the casing and then worked it out with pinchers, leaving a hole ready for noiseless insertion after everyone was asleep. Young Jules was told of my activities.

"I'll rip his belly open with my toadsticker!" he promised, flourishing his one-bladed knife.

"I'll— I'll— " But I could not say that my tactics were aggressive.

That evening our father was careful not to sit between the lamp and the unblinded window while he ate his supper. He found no relish in the accumulation of daily papers, no interest in the new *Geographic*, and contrary to all precedents, he went to bed early. Mother and I cleared away the dishes, but every crunching step outside brought our eyes fearfully together. A belated pig came grunting to the sill; the forgotten cat scratched against the door for her milk; even Keno, the pup, was gone, and I visualized him in the last convulsions of poisoning. Finally everyone was in bed.

When the house began to crackle as old frame houses do if one lies awake to hear, I sneaked out with the spike gripped in my hand. In my horror of being too late—of having the door pushed open in my face—I couldn't find the hole, and the spike slipped from my stiff fingers to the floor with a tremendous clatter.

"Jule!" our mother whispered to her spouse.

But Father was awake, whispering too. "Keep low, keep low," he commanded her, "so I dare shoot."

I was petrified; my legs like posts. They thought I was the killer! Should I let a probable prowler know my whereabouts? But the scrape of my father's rifle on the wall as he took it down decided me. Closing my eyes and gritting my teeth I took a dive into the unknown, expecting to stop lead either way.

"It's only me!"

No one kindly shot me. In utter disgrace I was packed off to bed and ordered to stay there, "or you'll get a hell of a licking!" Father threatened. Disgusted, I covered my head with the sheet and hoped we would all be killed.

The next morning even Keno made an appearance. Mother hoed under the trees near the house; the boys hung about, something very unusual for them; I puttered away at the housework, trying not to disturb Father lying on the lounge staring at the ceiling.

After dinner, while searching the cherry trees for ripening fruits, I glimpsed a horsebacker coming up through the young orchard. There was no road; only an occasional hunter from down the river came that way. Hard upon my announcement of his coming, the horseman trotted into the yard. It was the white-eyed man.

He swung from his saddle* and stopped, his right hand free over the revolver in his holster. Just then Father limped into the doorway, his rifle across his arm.

"How, Jule!" The man used the old settler's Indian greeting in a surly growl. If there was an answer to the greeting it escaped me. Under his shaggy brows, Father's eyes were sharp as gray gimlets, his palm caressing the grip of his rifle, his forefinger in the trigger guard. Behind him I could see Mother's blue dress and behind her the white faces of the boys.

"What you want?" Jules Sandoz asked the question always demanded of friend or foe.

"Just riding through—" The man's voice was insolent. "This is the road to Pine Creek, ain't it?" As if he had every right in our yard!

The two men's eyes held, riveted.

---

* While talking this over with the family for *Old Jules* later, we remembered that the man stayed on his horse.

"Yah!" Father spat, at last. "And take it—get off the place, and get damn quick!"

Slowly the man turned his back, mounting his horse deliberately, heavily. He held the impatient animal still, looking down upon the locator in the doorway, his hand resting on the butt of his revolver. Silence hung between them like a poised rattler. Almost imperceptibly Father's finger tightened on the trigger, the knuckles of his hand whitening.

With a laugh that was more a snarl, the man threw back his head, baring his teeth like a dog's. He jerked the reins and loped out of our yard, up the hill, and out of sight.

"They don't catch me unprotected," Father commented, lowering his gun. I went to bed with a sick headache.

A few weeks later we heard that an officer at Roswell, New Mexico, contrived to room with a man he suspected was the killer wanted in the hills. To make certain he tried that antique dodge, an uneasy conscience, exhibiting all the signs of relentless remorse. When the stranger asked him what the trouble was, he said that he had killed a man in a fight.

"Hell, that's nothing! I killed one in cold blood and you don't see me losing sleep over it!"

It all seemed too absurd, even then. The murderer, however, was actually captured there, returned, tried, found guilty of manslaughter, and sentenced to ten years in prison. With good behavior reductions he was out on parole before the bereaved family had adjusted themselves. Even so, the conviction was a definite homesteader victory. In the past these killers had trumped up some sort of case and escaped even temporary detainment.

And just when we settled back into some semblance of normalcy, Father announced that he had filed upon an additional three quarters, his lawful allotment, twenty-five miles away, over the rolling, terrible hills.

"You are crazy!" Mother lamented.

Not until we learned that a residence must be established did we children sense the full significance of the calamity. Father had put up a small shack and nailed the door shut to prevent the scum that rides the first wave of population into a new country from stealing everything movable. Early in September we set out for the shack. Due to the buckskins' temperamental behavior at gates or during Father's lapses into absent-mindedness, I was commandeered to go along, much to my discomfort. But audible objections were never in order from the Sandoz family, and so, with all the seriousness of an eleven-year-old with responsibilities, I gripped the lines; Father swung the whip; and the buckskins shot ahead. We were off, into the dreadful hills.

Heat, sand, lizards, and undulations that blended into a perfect similarity stretched endlessly before us. Even game was scarce. We saw few birds, no grays, no cattlemen, only one rattler, and that one escaped into a prairie-dog hole. We passed an occasional dugout, a little soddy, or an old claim shack, all dull gray and alone in russet or sandgrass valleys. Often we left the wagon trail, only two dim yellowish streaks over the darker tan or obliterated entirely by the light wind in the sand cuts, and struck across the hills. Toward noon the buckskins began to lag. First one singletree and then the other ground the wheel. Squinting under his cap at the sun, Father pulled up to a windmill, scattering a bunch of ruminating Herefords. The team was watered; we lunched from a tin cookie box; and then we went on. The hills grew higher; the valleys harder, re-sounding under the small hoofs. Soddies were more frequent, with here and there a long gray strip of late breaking, a few anaemic sunflowers pushing up between the sods.

About five o'clock we arrived at Pete's place, where a preliminary school meeting was in session. The half-soddy, half-frame house was filled with gaunt, sun-bronzed men and women. Several slightly gray girl-women, "Boston old maids" Father dubbed them, sat primly on improvised benches, squeezed in between women nursing babies and men chewing tobacco. Few of the men carried guns, although Pete, a second cousin, had a rifle hung on his wall. Someone told about a celebration given at the Spade ranch, with everything free for the settlers, including ice cream. Were the cattlemen following the gray wolves into mythology?

The next morning we bumped over trackless bunch-grass knolls and finally rattled down over a steep hill. In a high grassy valley, a tiny, new pine shack leaned against the south slope—our homestead. The buckskins snorted and fidgeted about approaching it.

"Hold 'em. I'll walk over," Father warned as he started to see if anything had been disturbed. Before I had the nervous team quieted, he came running back, bobbing grotesquely in his limp, his mouth to the back of his hand.

"Bit by a rattlesnake under the house while I reached for the hammer!"

The words came in jerks between spittings of clear saliva. The hills did a queer dance—bit by a rattlesnake—a rattlesnake! But Father pushed his pocket knife into my hand and jerked it away before I really could open it, and slashed at the large, purplish swelling about two pin-pricks. The dull blade sank into the puffy flesh but did not cut even the skin. With a groan he flung the knife from him and sucked fiercely.

"I may drop dead any minute!"

His eyes turned habitually to his constant companions in danger—his guns. He grasped the pump-gun.

"Hold that team!" he commanded. I gasped, but before I could form a coherent thought, he slapped his palm down on the rim of the hind wagon-wheel, laid the muzzle against the swelling, holding the gun steady between his body and the wagon bed. A shot echoed up and down the hills. The buckskins plunged ahead. I fell off the seat but clung to the lines. Bracing my feet against the dashboard, I pulled and jerked until the ponies slowed to a short lope, to a trot. When I finally turned them, Father was limping toward me. Black clotty blood dripped from the back of his hand where the swelling had been. I tied the lines about my waist, ripped the blue shirt sleeve, and made a handkerchief tourniquet just below the shoulder. Then, grayfaced, Father lay down in the wagon bed.

"Drive for Pete's and drive like hell!"

Too terrified to ask the direction, I swung the whip over the ponies, letting them take their heads. They sprang out; my sun-bonnet flew off; the board seat went next as we bounced over the bumpy knobs. I dared not look at the man in the wagon. I was afraid.

Foam from the ponies' mouths hit cold against my cheek. With my feet far apart, I hung to the lines as we tore at breakneck speed down a long hill and across a valley. It all seemed so strange, unreal. Surely this was not the way we came an hour ago, perhaps only fifteen minutes ago? We must be lost. And just when I was sure that we were, I saw the place. Pete came running out to stop what he considered just another runaway.

With his wife he helped Father into the house and then he ran to saddle a horse and ride to John Strasburger's homestead for whisky. I knew he was aggressively temperance; he would never have any. Even if he did, I had heard of a shepherder who died from snake bite while dead drunk. By the time that Pete came back, brandishing a tall bottle about a quarter full, Father's arm was purple to the shoulder. He gulped the brown liquid.

"It's not enough," he mumbled hopelessly, and sank back.

Pete ran to hitch his team to the top buggy. I held the horses while he went to fetch Father, staggering, but not drunk. "Don't let them run away," he warned as the buggy sagged under his weight. I thought he meant the buckskins. Hold horses, hold horses! Would I really have to drive home alone? They would run away; the gates were too hard to open; I could never find the way. . . .

Pete cut my introspections short by swinging me into the buggy bed at his feet. We shot through the yard gate and were on our way home. After four or five miles of sand the fiery team slowed, their lathered sides heaving. Father's face was sunken into his beard, his eyes closed. He swayed a little. I reached my arm around his knees and held on to the seat to keep him from sliding forward. Once he looked down upon me.

"Swelling's spreading into the lungs," he panted thickly. Pete whipped the jaded team into an unbelievably slow run.

"If he kills his team getting me home, tell Mama to pay for them," Father instructed me. I pulled my skirt up to my face and cried, slowly, hopelessly. "Your mama's a good woman," he went on, his breath wheezing. "And you'll get like her. Marry a farmer and help build up the country."

This unprecedented sentiment from our father disorganized any resistance I might have had. I must have wailed, for Pete cautioned me.

"Hush, you'll have to keep steady. We may need you to drive before this day is done."

Biting the gingham of my skirt—I'll always remember the taste of the cotton and the dye on my tongue—I calmed myself. After all, violence was a constant specter at our elbows. . . . But the sun burned my unshaded eyes. My head ached. And still the wheels spun yellow sand into my lap, my face. Father did not answer our inquiries any more. At two claim shacks we stopped. Only frightened faces rewarded us. No one had anything. At last we were in sight of the blue ribbon of the Niobrara. Pete whipped up the gaunt, lathered team and in one last spurt we were in our own yard.

"Ah, now, you let the horses run away!" Mother scolded as she ran out to meet us. But when she understood she sent me flying on cramped legs into the house for a cup of whisky, a big cup. Father shot it into his mouth. Before they had him in the house, I was on my way to Sears's, for of course our telephone was out of order! It was clear that I could make the mile trip in less time than Pete's horses, already down in their harness in the yard.

Dropping into a dog trot which previous emergencies had taught me I could hold for the mile, I finally lived to cover the infinite distance. And Bachelor Charley was an eternity answering my knock on the screen door.

Long after dark that night, as I lay abed in a coma from exhaustion, I was awakened by Young Jules shouting into my ear: "The doctor's come—in a red automobile!"

And so he had, but I didn't get to see the mechanical contrivance. A funny, short man pushed me back to my pillow, telling me I must be still. Father would pull through. But he might have been dead long before this from the deadly September venom if he hadn't shot it off.

Thus ended our plans to take up a new homestead that fall. In the winter Father changed his filing for a more promising one.

II

When the time for residence establishment on Father's homestead in the sandhills arrived, James, my second brother, and I were delegated to spend the summer and fall in the new shack. We were to live alone in the terrible hills with only a twenty-two rifle for protection. But I was glad. Perhaps the hills seemed a worthy antagonist. Perhaps I was already one with that strange land.

To Jules Sandoz, living alone like that was nothing, and we tried to imitate him. But when the buckskin team disappeared through the west pass toward our old home on the Niobrara twenty-five miles away, we looked at each other a little frightened. And in our ears rang Father's last command:

"Watch your fires, or you'll be burning the country out. Ranchers don't plow the guards like they used to. Remember those kids that burned in the Osborne—and look out."

We had nodded soberly, appreciating the danger. Our homestead was cut by the old dividing line between the Spade and the Springlake ranches. North of our frame shack the line guards, two strips of plowing approximately eight or ten feet wide and sixteen feet apart, trailed over knolls and through draws. They were weedy, neglected. South of our little strip of breaking the reddening bunchgrass waved unbroken. We roamed about these knolls, hunting rabbits and young grouse for our frying pan, seeing almost no one, and losing our vigilance about fires.

Then one morning a vague, iridescent veil hung along the horizon—a prairie fire.

"But it's far away," I consoled James, and myself.

The veil changed to piling billows of sulphurous yellow. The southeast wind freshened. Three heavy wagons filled with men rattled past, the Springlake hay crew going to fight the fire. Now and then a horsebacker galloped over the hills. One stopped at our shack.

"You kids better stay close to the breaking. Let the house and stuff burn. Lay face down on the plowing and you'll be all right."

So it was coming our way! The wind blew harder, trailing the pungent smoke in long, blue-black rolls over our heads. We tried to eat our dinner, but despite myself I kept talking about the three-month fire old-timers still recall. Only a heavy snowstorm had stopped that one. James, his blue eyes round, kept mentioning the two boys who had left their guard-protected sod house and ran into the swamp while their father and mother were away fighting the fire. They were burned to death in the tall rushes, only a mile north of our shack!

By two o'clock the smoke streamed along like a gray blanket just a few feet over our heads. We imagined red flames in the dark depths. Suddenly the strain of waiting was too much. We ran to the top of a hill, to another, and another. Only endless dunes and smoke. Even our little strip of breaking was lost.

While we stood, dumbfounded, a coyote tore past, not five feet away. Cattle bawled. We saw their flying feet below the smoke, heard the thunder of their hoofs. Now shouts cut the dull roar of wind and flames.

A gang plow broke from the smoke, almost upon us. A man was riding a horse in the lead, another was on the seat, hanging to the levers as the sod rolled out in ribbons. Behind them ran the "backfirers" scattering flames along the southeast side of the new guard. These little fires burned back into the wind very slowly, spreading along the guard and widening it materially. Singed men swung sacks and old chaps upon any backfire that got too vigorous. All worked frantically against time.

A curtain of flame shot up from the earth on a grassy knoll, crackling, leaping, The fire was upon us. We fled, as the cattle and the coyote had fled.

On a bare knoll we stopped, panting. The fire now was almost out. Cautiously we stole back to listen to the exploits of the day. Men were plodding wearily along the guard, beating out smoldering spots. Two groups closed in from the sides. They had tapered the fire and finally headed it, after contesting every step of the sixty miles between the starting spot near the railroad tracks and here. Then two women drove up with a cream can full of hot coffee. One of them, the music teacher, was vastly interested in the many settlers left homeless in that sixty mile strip. Grateful that the fire had been turned from her "Pleasant Home," she asked us who we were, and gave us cookies.

Thrillingly the memory of all this came back to me as I stood before the ruins of her old house and rubbed the velvety surface of the sign. I had almost forgotten the little woman, yet she had helped make the long months before Mother moved into the district less lonesome by sending me little notes and verses about the "purpled hills" and the "baptismal silences." And she had loaned me the novels of Conrad. How could I have forgotten that!

But she represented only one type of the strange folk we found in the sandhills. Coming from every corner and blind alley of the world, the settlers were sure to differ in their conception of a fitting mode of life and habitation. Some lived in their wagons or in the open, until the winter's early march forced them to dig into the ground. Hay from a rancher's meadow formed the roof of their dugouts and the pallets in the corners, and even filled the round barrel of the hay burners that smoked furiously and reddened the eyes. An occasional foreigner and his wife, refugees from a more bitter foe than cold or loneliness, lived content in a dugout for several years. Many an erratic bachelor, lacking the proddings of ambitious women folk, lived in the ground until a wandering range cow or his own horse fell unheralded into the dark and damp interior. Then there was the drifter who built himself a winter lodge of old rushes held together with barbed wire and posts pilfered from a rancher's hay corral. The penniless ate veal, stealthily but surely. And the cattlemen, suddenly " on the wrong side of the fence," could do nothing.

The music teacher, a little afraid of the rough-appearing men who rode past or stopped for a drink at her well, continued to live alone. Contrary to all predictions by the rougher women, she grew ruddy of skin; she liked the wind-ruffled grass about her door, the whistling curlew on a knoll, the yellow-breasted meadow lark singing his morning song on her plank pump, and the purples and yellows of the hills. The women who had sniffed at her ideas welcomed her when there was sickness or when a new baby came to a mother who needed coaxing to take up the weary burden once more.

Another kind of settler was the prosperous one who "shipped in" from Tulsa or Elmhill, or Cotter's Corners. Livery freighters planted dressers, incubators, cream separators, and rocking chairs on the bare prairie and went away. With the awkward breaking plow the man turned up smooth ribbons of gray earth in a low spot where the sod was densely rooted. With the help of the entire family a soddy was put up in two or three days. Plastered with gray mud from an alkali lake bed, it was cosy. Let the winter winds howl, the summer sun bake.

Different as these Kinkaiders were, we found them united by a common bond. Two of them, in fact. All these settlers wanted a railroad; held meetings, consumed enormous amounts of chewing tobacco, and went home optimistic. Nothing came of it. The other was, as most bonds

are, a common need. Fuel. With no tree closer than the
Niobrara River or the brush of the Snake, with little
money and wretched roads over twenty to forty miles of
sun-drenched or snow-glazed hills to the nearest railroad,
wood and coal were out of the question. Cow-chips were
the solution. Most of the settlers had lost all the qualms
that curse the fastidious long before they reached the hills.
Barehanded they took up the battle, braving rattlesnakes
which, upon acquaintance, failed to live up to their reputation for aggressiveness. City women incased their still-
white hands in huge gloves and, with a repugnance no
extremity could completely erase, endured the first few
weeks somehow. The music teacher wore gloves to the
very last.

The first winter always brought the most squeamish to
a proper appreciation of this cheap and practical solution
to the heating problem. We forgot that we could not saw
down a tree if our fuel ran short in midwinter, and after
only two months of moderately cold weather our house
was so frigid that we wore old coats in the kitchen and the
baby was swathed like an Eskimo. The winter was un-
usually open and warm, as some wag said everyone's first
winter in a new country always is. The cattle that were to
pay off the $1,700 mortgage coming due in the fall had
survived fairly well on nothing except a bit of corn fodder
and range. Now the faint green of spring was on the hills.
The last day of April brought a warm rain; it turned to
snow by night.

"Three foot of snow by morning," Father predicted,
voicing a standing exaggeration joke of the hills, but one
just a bit too near the truth for unadulterated humor. The
next morning Mother tunneled out of the door with the
fire shovel and followed the yard fence to the windmill,
as invisible in the flying snow as if it were in the Antarctic
instead of fifteen yards from the house. The wind screeched

and howled. Mother didn't return. Had she taken the wrong fence from the tank, the one that led off into the pasture? Just when I was mustering the courage to awaken the family, she came back, white, snow-covered from head to foot, her eyelashes grizzled with ice.

"The cattle are gone!" she announced, exploding her bomb with characteristic abruptness. She had been to the shed and they had evidently drifted with the storm, to stumble into snowbanks, to chill into pneumonia, to smother, to freeze. With them went our home on the Niobrara, our start in cattle in the hills, even our team, successors to the buckskins, mortgaged for the interest.

That May Day was a gloomy one. We foraged along the fence, tearing out alternate posts to chop up on the kitchen floor with the hatchet. No one was permitted out of the door without being tied to a rope. The lamp burned all day.

The next morning, long before daylight, Mother awakened Young Jules and me. The wind was dead; the stars were out; and the shed was empty of everything except Blackie and Brownie, nickering for feed. They were saddle-broken and on them we were to trace our cattle, dig out and save what we could. After gulping a hot breakfast we were bundled into most of the clothing the family possessed. Mother wrapped an endless fascinator about my tender head. Climbing upon the old horses, we set out, equipped with a spade and a hammer.

Daylight stalked cold and gray over the knolls as we crunched into the frozen snow. About two hundred yards from the house we found a cow, up to her neck in a drift, her eyes already white—mad. Mother waved us on. She would salvage that one. From the top of a wind-cleared knoll, we looked across the valley, lightening into a pure sheet of white. Not quite pure, for here and there were dark heads, moving or still, along the dim snow trail.

With true horse sense, Brownie smelled out the drifts that held her up. If she or Blackie broke through into the bottomless drifts, there was nothing to do but scoop a path to a knoll or another crusted drift. The first few "critters" we reached were range cattle—Herefords, evidently from the Springlake herd that had drifted past our shed and tolled our cows away.

By the time we were on the hill half a mile from home, the sun shimmered on the endless field of spotless white. Mother had dug the cow out; her blackish hulk lay free in the glare. Over the ridge of hills toward the south the trail was blown clearer; here and there a track was visible, the crusted snow carved into fantastic sculpture or trailing white behind the soapweeds. We found several range cows, thin and exhausted, lying flat, and one of our calves, only his starred forehead out of a drift, dead.

The sun began to burn our faces. Perspiration, aroused by the shoveling, chilled us when we stopped on a hilltop to plan. There must be a trail for the return of whatever we might save.

The Strasburger homestead was scarcely discernible, house and barn little more than hummocks of snow. At least three hours gone to travel a mile and a half! In the next valley we found one of our cows up to her neck in snow and "on the prod" as the sandhiller would say. We dug her out, changing off on the spade and keeping a sharp eye out for the long horns. The snow was softening. We were wet to our hips. And when the cow was free and could stumble about a little on her frost-numbed legs, she rushed headlong at Jules and was stuck again. In disgust we left her and rode on.

The next one we found was dead. And still we climbed on and off our horses, digging, sweating, our feet clumpy and wooden with cold. Noon came. My face burned; my lips were blistering in the unprotecting fascinator. I wished vaguely for the smoked glasses at home in Mother's trunk. Jules, more protected by natural skin tone and a huge cap, was hungry. But there was little time for physical discomforts. A neighbor who was digging out a saddle horse caught in a draw shouted to us.

"You kids better get for home!" He said more but it was lost in the snow echo. We couldn't stop. Cattle that stayed in the snow much longer would be hopelessly chilled, probably be dead by morning. So we whipped the tired, sore-kneed horses on; threw snow left and right when the need arose. Our shoulders were numb now. They had ceased aching long ago.

About four o'clock, in a choppy range, we found the cattle. First three head, then five, other small bunches, jammed together by high drifts, unable to move. They bawled as we approached. At last, about six o'clock, we had them all free and had lost only the two cows along the way and the dead calf. The animals were gaunt; their skins jerked like palsied hands from cold, but they could walk, which was more than most of the range cattle could do.

Slowly we started homeward, not daring to push the cows for fear of their plunging into drifts or slipping and being unable to rise. I carried a new little calf, still damp and curly, across my saddle. Thanks to our day of pain, the trip home was short. Darkness came on gradually and there was joy in our yard when the bawling string trailed, single file, up to the shed. But we were beyond praise. We literally fell from our horses and were taken into the house with a solicitude entirely new to us. My head ached; we were starved, chilled; and the house was dark.

"Why don't you light the lamp?" I demanded.

Mother made a funny, gurgling noise. "Ah-h," her voice choked. "The lamp is lit. You are blind!"

Before morning I was delirious with pain and sunburn

fever. Scorching pinwheels whirled in my head. Father gave me a small dose of morphine to quiet my screams, and when that wore off, another. But he dared not give me any more. My eyes burned like seething, bubbling lead. My head seemed tremendously large, bursting. My face itched. I tore at my skin, so burned that it peeled off in strips like tissue paper. I could not eat nor sleep. And when the pain began to die down into a dull, monotonous ache, I, who was never still without a book, was a most impossible patient. The few people who found time to come in suggested all sorts of neglected precautions. I should have worn a black veil or smudged my cheekbones with soot. They talked of crippling cattle losses. Whole herds scattered like ours had died because they became chilled. One rancher lost over two hundred head piled into draws and smothered. Another lost five hundred head of stock in one lake. We, evidently, were fortunate.

At last I could find my way about to peel potatoes, carry water from the well, and do odd jobs about the house. The slightest infiltration of light under my bandage maddened me with pain. And when I finally took my bandage off, I found I could aim a gun without closing my left eye. It was blind.

The settlers suffered little from the late blizzard. Few of them had the money to stock their sections; they leased their land to the ranchers. Father tried to get them to farm. He argued that where sunflowers grow man-high, corn will also grow; that land which grows well-rooted sod only five to fifteen feet above ground-water with no intervening rock strata will grow alfalfa; that the northern slopes covered with chokecherries and wild plum thickets would grow tame fruit. Rye and corn proved reasonably successful. Crops brought better homes, more space, deep window seats with red geraniums, and perhaps tinted walls to suit the fancy of the girls becoming educated through the mail order catalogues, the Kinkaiders' "bible." But the homes like music boxes remained as they were, for the $100 annual rent permitted no luxuries.

Prosperity, unless it becomes too great, brings neighborliness. Where once each little shack curled pungent blue smoke from its stovepipe, now wagons, buggies, and saddle horses were grouped about a home on Sundays for a community dinner. Pure democracy excluded only the fat old widows who were afraid of horses and could not "hoof it." The music teacher was always remembered by someone who "could just as well swing 'round that way."

Out of the growing prosperity came the cattlemen's decision that these people actually intended to stay. No one seemed to starve. Father had a fifty-acre field of Turkistan alfalfa, and his orchard was doggedly growing in the white sand. The rising price of grass-fed stock on the Omaha market brought an offer for a good hay flat here and there. The offers became general. Kinkaiders who had never seen so much money before took their thousand dollars and wrote glowing letters to us. The grass grew wonderfully green in Cotter's Corners or in Hutton's Bottoms. Here and there a music box stood empty, the ruffly curtains gone, the owner glad, for the moment, that she was no longer compelled to live by herself. But our music teacher was loyal. With an old organ bought at Rushville, she gave music lessons. Her house should not be moved to a ranch for a tool shed! Boldly Father withstood the buyer when he came with an offer remarkably generous then, but not so generous now when I can appreciate the significance of his experiments. Yet our hearts beat just a little faster at the wonderful stories the letters told.

Then came the Bad Winter; unrivaled, old-timers told us, by any ever seen in the hills. On Election Day the first white flakes began to fall, fell every day until Thanksgiving, until Christmas. Disappointed children were told that Santa Claus was snowbound, but that Easter would be green and lovely and perhaps the Easter rabbit. . . . By Easter there was desperation in many homes. The usual January thaw, with frozen roads for coal hauling, did not materialize. Old hay burners were dug up and smoked the tinted walls, the oatmeal paper. Starving cattle bawled and then were still. No horse could plow far through the valleys. Illness, caused by long confinement, restricted diet, and discouragement over mortgaged cattle dying, was present in almost every home.

The first week in May brought the sun and summer winds. Snow water filled the valleys and the cellars, drowning out the alfalfa. This was the buyer's opportune moment. The music teacher, weak from a severe cold, was one of the first to sell. The shrewder, the more courageous, sensed the promise of the latent hills and mortgaged their claims to buy out their neighbors. Sod walls gaped open to the sun, making good rubbing places for the cattle, lousy from lowered vitality. But we scarcely noticed the Kinkaiders go, so busy were we with the extra work of Father's new orchard. To us it was not a general movement, an exodus; only the Wests, the Tuckers, and the Wyants went. I missed them, especially the music teacher. I missed her books. She had cried, just a little, the day she went away.

"But it's four miles to the Zimmers'—and six to the next neighbor's—and I—" she choked a sob into a fine old lace handkerchief. "It's no use—I'm afraid of dying alone."

Quickly she put her arms about my shoulders, kissed my unaccustomed cheek, and then climbed into the mail wagon.

The years piled up and I went away too, and now, after ten years of absence, there are only the weeds and the stove. As the mail truck moved on, we passed old cylinder holes,

almost filled, often with a piece of galvanized pipe still
sticking up. All that is left of an optimistic venture. Long
grayish streaks, grassed over, show where corn, rye, and
alfalfa once grew and will grow again. For there is Father's
orchard, the most talked-about spot in the State, to show
the skeptic what can be done.

And there are the prosperous ones who stayed, ranchers
now, their range deeded, safe from homesteaders and
fence-cutting troops. Where once each valley held its own
peculiar little home, now ten, fifteen miles reveal nothing
except fat cattle, windmills, and haystack-dotted mead-
ows. There are few fences and the truck does not stop
for these, bumping over pipe and cement contraptions
called "corduroy bridges." Families who started twenty
years ago in dugouts today have huge homes of fifteen
rooms, high-powered family cars, Fords for hack driving,
and radios. Sons and daughters are home from college, or
abroad for the summer. Their parents can choose between
Florida and California for wintering. The terrors of stalking man and beast, of cold and of loneliness, are gone—
for those who stayed. Who can say how those who are
gone have fared?

Each year finds the old home sites more nearly obliterated. The next storm will tear down from the rusty nail
the little teacher's sign with its brave legend. It will fall
into the sand and become a part of the hills, as will also the
memory of the dear woman who so carefully lettered it,
wherever she may be.

Musky

When Father drove his buckskin ponies out of the valley and left us alone on his new homestead, twenty-five miles from the rest, I kicked a loose sod as nonchalantly as I could. My brother James spit into the dust. Father was a frontiersman, a locator and trapper. Staying alone in the wilderness of sandhills and rattlesnakes meant nothing to him. But I was only thirteen, James younger. Before Father was out of sight we ran to the shack for the twenty-two rifle and climbed to the top of the south hill to look around.

During the hot days of August we saw scarcely a cowboy. Mostly just meadow larks, grouse, perhaps a dun coyote against the morning hillside. There were no near neighbors, so we spent our time hunting in the hills and the drying swamp of the valley over the hill north, or watering the few scrawny cabbages in the lower corner of the ragged breaking about our shack. Now and then we saw a rattlesnake under a tilted sod, found coiling tracks about our shallow-dug well, or caught the faint smell of dead things that clings to the haunts of the diamondback. I knew about rattlers. I had been in the hills once before, alone with Father, the time he was struck on the back of the hand by one. I still dreamed about that day, especially here in the pitch-piny shack with holes for windows and the door, sleeping on the ground, in the center of the breaking.

One night I awoke in a cold sweat, the blood pounding in my ears. Something scaly and cold moved slowly across my neck. I had to let it, and every moment I expected the punctures of fangs from a flat, arrow-shaped head.

I listened. There was not a sound. Even James, rolled in a blanket a few feet away, seemed not to breathe, as though already dead. And somewhere in the dark was the cold body, the poised head. The blackness of the room began to shimmer in fiery spots, pressing down, choking me. At last I had to breathe, and with the sound of a ripsaw through the stillness. There was no movement anywhere. Nothing except the faint smell of dead things.

Two feet away was the lantern, and matches, and along my arm lay the warm barrel of the rifle. But these things were as nothing—for somewhere, near my face, near my eyes, perhaps, was the cold scaly body of a snake. A move and there would be a whirr, a strike. Suddenly the darkness went spotty again. I was already bitten. My arm was numb, cold. It was spreading.

Then something cold touched my cheek, not piercingly, as with poisoned needles, but daintily, as the lick of a black tongue.

From there on I don't remember much, except that I lay tense and unmoving for as long as it took to build up all the layers of the earth under me. Gradually I became conscious of someone whispering.

"Mari, Mari—" very softly.

It was James, but I dared not answer. For the thing that had touched me had not moved away. When my brother's whispers veered from fright to horror, I answered, out of the far corner of my mouth. So we lay, listening, our eardrums almost splitting. But there was nothing to hear except the faint sound of quarreling water birds in the swamp, the occasional deep call of the thunder-pumper, the sudden sharp howl of a coyote on the knoll. At that there was a faint swishing sound at my ear and then nothing more.

Daylight came at last and the familiar things took form —the stove, the homemade table, the bench, finally the ridges in the dirt floor and James' drawn, frightened face. Cautiously I lifted my blanket. Nothing. But there, between us, were many tracks as of a finger drawn back and forth in graceful curves on the rough ground.

We slipped into our shoes and before dressing looked about the shack, even upsetting the cowchips from the fuel box. At last we settled down to breakfast.

Suddenly James made the queerest noise, dropped his fork, and ran to the corner where our old broom stood. A black, flattish tail and a brown, furry bunch showed on one side of it and on the other side a bit of dark nose and whiskers. James jerked the broom away. Cowering in the corner was a muskrat, two-thirds grown, pulled together in a shaking lump of frightened brown fur. So that was the cold tail that trailed over my neck; his whiskers, not a snake's tongue, had touched my cheek. We leaned against each other in foolish relief and laughed until the little fellow scurried away under the wall, where he had probably been all the time we were looking for him. But he was soon back behind the broom.

By dinner time we had Musky, as we called him, eating before us, nibbling with his bright yellow teeth at the thick roots we dug for him in the swamp. When we spoke to him he stood up tall and sniffed but returned to his food.

By evening we had put up a sod pen about three feet high, with the top link of our stove-pipe, which kept blowing off anyway, buried in the ground for a burrow and a nest from a rat house in the swamp in the far end. We built a little pond lined with alkali mud and fringed it with rushes, cattails, and arrow-heads. But Musky ran back and forth, trying to get out.

"Let's let him go," I suggested, half-heartedly, because our backs ached and our hands were blistered.

About dark he let James push him into the stove-pipe with the spade handle, but only a little way. After all, we couldn't tamp him into his hole as you would soil about a post.

Before we rolled up in our blankets we took the lantern out but couldn't find Musky. The next morning he was gone; nothing left of him but a hole between the sods. We were suddenly very lonely and a little angry too at his lack of appreciation. James walked through the browning marsh grass to our dried water-hole, calling, "Musky, Musky." I fried pancakes.

And then while we ate he came out from behind the broom. Our enthusiastic reception frightened him into a lope through the doorway but we headed him and drove him back into the house. Once more he settled behind the broom, his bright eyes watching. After an hour or two of apparent neglect he sallied forth to smell the bit of pancake we dropped for him.

Musky was curious and liked to explore the legs of the table, the stove, the chip-box, standing up and reaching as high as he could with his queer handlike forefeet. Once he stuck his nose against the hot ash-pan I lifted from the stove. He gave a sharp little squeak and loped away to his broom, wriggling his nose. There he rubbed it with his paw and looked at me from hurt eyes. The next morning he was gone.

"You went and let him burn himself!" James complained.

"Aw—can't he learn to keep out of the way?" I demanded in sisterly resentment. But I spent several hours searching for tracks like the insertion on my Sunday petticoat, a strip of graceful curving like ribbon in the center. That was his tail. The regular, dainty little spots on each side were the tracks of his feet. But the wind had rippled the surface of the sandpass leading to the swamp. I gave it up and went home to put the shack in order. We were expecting Father. James took the twenty-two and went out alone, pretending to look for game.

And then all at once Musky was in the doorway, wrinkling his nose in the air. Satisfied that he was welcome, he slid in and plodded to his corner. He was round as a ball, his sides sticking out like a bloated cow's. For the first time he let me pick him up. He even snuggled down in my arms and went to sleep. There was a scabby place on his shoulder, with a little dried pus, probably an old battle wound. From this came that dead smell I caught the night he trailed his tail over my neck and pushed his whiskers gently in my face. I sopped the scab with a solution of carbolic acid and let him sleep curled up in the corner.

That evening Father came, with Jule, our eldest brother. We tried to coax Musky out to nibble crumbs but he was shy and aloof. Probably not hungry. Anyway he took one look at the newcomers and scurried to the door.

"Head him off!" Father ordered, but Musky slipped between my awkward feet.

"Oh, now you let him get away. His hide is green yet but he'd bring fifteen, twenty cents."

James and I looked at each other. Of course our trapper father would look at it like that. Jule took the lantern out but came back alone.

"We'll set a trap for him. He may come back," Father said over his pipe.

There wasn't much we could do. Remonstrances were out of order in our family, but a little subterfuge was not. When the rest were in bed I slipped out and listened. It was September, chilly, and the rattlesnakes were holed up for the night. So I slipped through the breaking. Down at the lower edge of the garden plot I heard a soft gnawing that stopped every time I moved. Probably Musky in the cabbages. I sat down and called softly. The noise stopped completely and after a long time I felt something like fluff along my stocking and a cold nose against my hand. He let me carry him to the house and put him into an empty nail keg. There he was, a round, brown ball, when I crossed the frosty yard the first thing the next morning.

By the next evening we got permission to snap the number one steel trap set along the door. Father decided he might as well wait until the fur was prime.

That day he tacked in the windows and hung the door. Jule tried to make friends with Musky but the little chap's affections couldn't be forced. When our impatient brother tried to make him nibble at a root as he did for us, Musky bared his yellow teeth and snapped them on Jule's finger. He almost died for his daring. James rescued him and ran away, the frightened little head buried under his arm. When we were alone again he learned to trust us almost as before. He still slept behind the broom and foraged about the room at night, his long digger nails making a loud noise on our new floor. On cold nights he snuggled in at James' feet. Sometimes he tried trailing along when we went hunting but he couldn't understand this climbing the towering sandhills and after the first pitch he usually gave up and plodded back to the cabbages and the sod corn or waited outside the door until we came to open it.

Musky made few noises with his mouth. Once or twice when I stepped too close to him he gave the funny cry of the day he sniffed the hot ash-pan. And once when a coyote howled daringly close to the house he cried like that outside the door and scratched frantically until we let him in to be safe in our companionship.

He was less and less interested in the roots we brought from the swamp, preferring to chew on the loose nubbins from our corn fodder or on a bit of cabbage. Snow fell.

Musky's fur got thick and close and grayer, but still a little
shaggy, not glossy as that of his kind in the cold swamp.
He got fatter and softer, too, and when Mother came down
with the household goods and the babies she found him in
the cowchip box behind the stove.

"Out you go!" she commanded. "No, I won't have
animals like that in my house. Couldn't you catch a badger
or maybe a skunk or two?" She chased Musky out into
the dark with the old broom that had sheltered him so
often. It was sad.

But the next day we found that he had made a nest behind an anchor post of the windmill set up on the new well
that took the place of the old spade-dug hole, now covered
with a few boards and hay so the children wouldn't fall
into it. Musky seldom came to the house after that but he
got his cabbage hearts and corn, and he drank at the chicken
trough. And often I was scolded for spending my time
scratching his jolly soft sides and pulling his fat cheeks
when I should have been minding babies. Sadly I gave up
my free ways of the last few months. My *Wanderjahr* was
over.

But James was loyal and even Jule fed Musky now and
then. Father scratched his beard and laughed as he told us,
prophetically, how much he would get for the hide.

When winter was upon us we carried home sacks of hay
and, with manure over it to generate heat, made a house
for Musky. He trotted out to the chicken coop to eat and
drink, and, while the rooster was suspicious, the hens
ignored him. But somehow he seemed a little neglected
and sad now. I hoped he would make the break and run
away, not to the north swamp, however, for Father was
chopping into the freezing rat houses and setting traps.

Then one day as I poured steaming water into the frozen
chicken trough, Musky didn't come. I hadn't noticed him
for several days. Neither had the boys.

"Now you let him get away," Father said, but even he didn't seem to be so very sorry.

The winter was cold but short and February brought a fine thaw with snow-water running. It washed away the hay from the old well and Mother decided it must be filled. Something floated about on the surface. We dipped a bucket under it. Musky. The call to water had become too strong for him.

His hair was slipping and so we buried him in the dead cabbage patch. James almost cried for this foolish little Musky who deserted his fine swamp and his gay fellows for a corner behind the old broom, some cabbage hearts, and two stupid children. And I didn't share James' boyish fear of shedding honest tears.

The Son

In regard to the origin of my social consciousness, the members
of my father's family were followers of Pedro Waldo in his
pre-Reformation rebellion against the tyranny and corruption
of the church. When the executions and recantations began,
our family fled from Lombardy to France, and when the
religious persecutions became too intense there, they crossed
over into Switzerland, where a branch of our family partici-
pated actively in the progressive legislation that made Switzerland, at the end of the nineteenth century, a model for new
nations.

The members of my mother's family were from the Canton
of Schwyz and took an active role in the formation of the
original confederation of Uri, Schwyz, and Unterwalden in
1291, from which emerged the Confederation of Switzerland.

My own liberalism came from this fertile past as well as
from a childhood of living in the midst of poverty. A continual
caravan of the world's disinherited passed by our house in
quest of free lands which my father helped them to find.
Among them there was also the constant recognition of the
exploitation of the Western states by the loan-bankers of the
East. All of this we heard talked about in our childhood as well
as the history of rapacious empires—of the expansion of Rome
to all Europe, the expansion of Spain in the New World, the
expansion of England all over the globe—and the expansion

of the United States, which already at that time resembled England in its use of military power and financial capital.

Thus, having at an early age become aware of the long struggle to obtain and defend a small and decent portion of individual liberty, and of the recent pressures against this liberty—as society became more and more complex—the development of my social consciousness was logically inevitable. Moreover, there was another determining factor in my childhood: the daily presence of an expropriated race, the American Indian. I was attracted to them very much, as children are always attracted by men of grand bearing, graciousness, and wisdom. One of the greatest of these, old He Dog, brother chieftain of the great Crazy Horse, called me his granddaughter until he died around 1937. From him and others like him, I developed a feeling of the brotherhood with all the things on earth which is the essence of the ancient philosophy of the Sioux, and the foundation of the deep sense of responsibility which each Sioux feels for each member of his community.

One morning the summer I was eight a small playmate from the Indian camp across the road came to tap shyly at our kitchen door, motioning to me.

"Ahh! I have a brother too now!" she whispered, her dark eyes on the baby astride of my hip. "He is just born. Come see!"

I pushed the oatmeal to the back of the stove and hurried out as fast as I could, holding my brother close as I ran. He laughed and shouted, bobbing heavily on my hip, already so big that we seemed like some wobbling, double-headed creature. But I slowed up at the smoky old canvas tipi, shy too, now, as I looked into the dusky interior where an Indian woman bent over the new baby on her lap.

At the noise of our excitement, the tiny red-brown face began to pucker up tighter. But the mother caught the little nose gently between her thumb and forefinger, and with her palm over the mouth, stopped the cry soundlessly. When the baby began to twist for breath she let go a little, but only a little, and at the first sign of another cry, she shut the air off again, crooning a soft little song to the child as she did this, a Cheyenne growing song to make the son straight-limbed, and strong of body and of heart.

I watched the mother enviously. Although our baby was a year old and able to run if I had the time to play with him, he rode my hip most of his waking hours, except when he was fed or when our mother was home from the field or the orchard and could sit down a moment. Otherwise he howled, and our father was not the man to tolerate a crying baby.

I already knew why none of my small Indian friends made more than a whimper at the greatest hurt. An old grandmother had told me that Indian mothers always shut off the first cry of the new-born, and as often after that as necessary to teach this first, this greatest lesson out of the old Indian life: No one can be permitted to endanger the people; no cry must guide a skulking enemy to the village or spoil a hunt that might mean the winter's meat for a whole tribe.

But I knew too that never, in the natural events of this small boy's life, would he be touched by a punishing hand. Somehow he would be made equal to the demands of his expanding world without any physical restriction beyond the confines of the cradleboard, and no physical punishment. I remember the stern, distant faces of the Sioux when, in the swift heat of his temper, our father whipped us. These Indians still consider the whites a brutal people who treat their children like enemies—playthings, too, coddling them like pampered pets or fragile toys, but underneath always like enemies, enemies that must be restrained, bribed, spied upon, and punished. They believe

that children so treated will grow up as dependent and
immature as pets and toys, and as angry and dangerous as
enemies within the family circle, to be appeased and
fought. They point to the increasing lawlessness and violence of our young people, so often against their elders, a
thing unheard of among these Indians.

Our brown-skinned neighbors had a traditional set of
precautions against such immaturities and resentments.
They tried to avoid any overprotection of the young, particularly the mother's favoritism for the eldest son as we
saw it all around us, a favoritism that aroused our own
father's anger, and not assuaged by our mother's long
practice of hurrying the first-born son away from any
punishment. Even so it was better in our home than in
most because our father took his sons hunting, trapping,
and on surveying trips. He let them have guns and traps
almost from infancy, showed them how to use these well
and safely. He let the eldest drive the wild team while he
sat on the seat beside him and talked of the early days as to
another adult.

Yet even so there was enough anger between the father
and his first-born son to drive the boy away to his uncle
at fourteen, not to return for four years, and then as a
towering, laughing young man who could make light of
his mother's coddling anxieties and his father's resentments.

Our Indian friends, out of their long years in the close
confines of skin lodges, winter and summer, understood
these natural conflicts. A continent people, they usually
spaced their children so no woman was encumbered with
more than one child too small to run if they must flee from
an enemy or a buffalo stampede. Yet a prolonged infancy
was recognized as fatal to a proper maturing and a good
orientation into the life of the community, particularly for
the eldest son, who was derisively called "the little husband" if he tagged at his mother's moccasins. The Indians

understood the resentment that could grow up in the most tolerant, fortitudinous man if he saw his wife's affection and attention turned to his son, and they appreciated too a badly reared boy's jealousy of his mother.

So, by custom, the eldest son was provided with a second father, usually a man with a warmhearted wife at whose fireside the boy would spend a great deal of time and whom he could treat with less formality than his own mother. The second father selected for the boy born across the road from our house was an uncle, and the man's white teeth flashed in the sunshine with as much happy pride as the actual father. If later the boy should show some special bent, he might select still another man, one fitted to guide these new interests. Once it was perhaps a fine warrior, a hunter, arrowmaker, holy man, or an artist and band historian. Now it would perhaps be a good farmer, a cattleman, rodeo rider, mechanic, office worker, athlete, artist, engineer, or perhaps a doctor, from a long line of healers.

The young Indian's relationship to his mother-in-law was even more carefully circumscribed. Unless already an important chief, the new groom left his people for his wife's, sometimes to live within the close confines of the same skin lodge with the girl's mother, or a one-room reservation shack. To avoid the tensions and conflicts, respectful conduct required that both the husband and the mother-in-law address each other only through a third person, never directly. Even if they sat across the table from each other three times a day it was the ultimate in disrespect to let their eyes meet. I recall a gay, gregarious young Sioux who liked to visit with the family of his girl friend as much as he liked taking her to dances. But the marriage stopped his pleasant gossipy visits with her mother, until he maneuvered his new wife into a divorce. The next day he had returned to her mother's kitchen, chair tilted back, passing the time.

I have never known a case of mother-in-law trouble among the Cheyennes or even the Sioux, whose women are a little more assertive than some, perhaps because they recall the days, not so distant, when the lodge belonged to the woman and if her husband displeased her too much she might throw his regalia out into the village circle and all he could do was pick it up shamefacedly, and lug it to his mother's lodge.

My youngest brother was born with a hernia that might be aggravated by crying. At six weeks it was completely healed but the damage was done. He was rotten spoiled. I knew that an Indian mother would probably have controlled his crying without danger, considering the Indians' expert management of hernia, and so I looked with increasing envy from the boy on my hip to the new baby across the road, sleeping so quietly and sweetly in his cradleboard. With him handy at her elbow, the mother went about her work, perhaps beading moccasins or belts and bags for the white-man stores along the railroad. But the boy must be free to try his legs and to get his discipline in the natural way, through experience and from his peers, as he must be free to take his ideals and aspirations from the precepts and examples of his elders. So the dark-eyed little Indian was out of the cradleboard for long hours, lying contentedly on a blanket while the other children of the camp played around him and someone tended the little sweetgrass smudge to keep the flies and mosquitoes away.

Here the boy heard the shouts and laughing of the children, the talk of the camp, of the formal evening smoke, and the counciling. But he heard no quarrels. Repeated dissension within the village circle brought ostracism among both the Sioux and the Cheyennes, and only too much white-man whisky will make an Indian break this old, old taboo today. Nor would the new baby hear loud voices in his mother's dwelling, and as a good son he would never speak loudly or rudely in her presence. But early he would learn the power of chastising laughter, whether at the quiet fireside, on the playground, or against those in the highest position. Even great war leaders have bowed in humiliation before concerted public laughter.

When the Indian boy began to crawl no one would cry, "No, no!" and drag him back from the enticing red of the fire. Instead, his mother or anyone near would watch only that he did not burn up. "One must learn from the bite of the flame to let it alone," he would be told as he jerked his hand back, whimpering a little, and with tear-wet face brought his burnt finger to whoever was near for soothing. The boy's eyes would turn in anger not toward his mother or any grownup who might have frustrated his desire, but towards the pretty coals, the source of his pain. He would creep back another time, but slower, warily, and soon know where warmth became burning.

By the time he was six weeks old he had learned about water. "He must go into the river before he forgets the swimming," the mother told me, an ability she was certain was given to the young of all creatures alike: the pup, the colt, the buffalo calf, the child. The boy swam well before he could walk, and so it was safe to let him play around the placid river when they came visiting again the next summer. If he fell in he could paddle and grab at the grass of the bank. He had learned to walk stalking up and down on the belly of one or the other of his fathers, the man flat on his back, holding the boy up with his hands and laughing at the sturdy thrust of the young legs. He fell into cactus and rosebrush and learned to pull the thorns out or hobble to the other children for help.

I watched this year-old Indian boy who could look after himself as a puppy would, or a colt, and then upon the brother who still clung to my hip, two years old, and heavy as stone. I set him down and when he howled I whipped him until my hand stung, and every time that our parents were away I repeated this, until he learned to look around before he opened his mouth, grinning sheepishly at me if we were alone, and then impishly, good-natured. It was hoeing time, a busy time, and in two, three weeks he was well along to a cure, but there was a day or two when I had trouble sitting down.

The boy across the road was learning too that there are acceptable patterns of conduct and some that are not, perhaps from the long heroic tales told at every fireside, and from the example of his elders, but surely from the sting of laughter or another boy's fist in his face. Gradually he discovered how to avoid some of the laughing and blows, or to fend them off. One of his grandfathers had been a wrestler and was very useful in the fending. Mostly, however, the boy learned from those a few years older, as later he passed on what he knew. The Indians believed that discipline from those who are young too comes as from the earth, and is accepted as naturally as hunger and weariness and the bite of winter cold, without the resentment aroused by commands from grownups, from the big and the over-powering. True, the laughter, the rule of his peers was at times unjust. It was an unjust world in which the boy must live, a world where lightning strikes the good man as well as the bad, where sickness respects no virtue, and luck flits from this one to that as vagrantly as the spring butterfly. The realization that injustice exists and must be met with resistance where possible, tolerated where necessary, comes with less bitterness to the very young.

The boy from across the road learned about sex in the natural way too, early enough so the meaning came to him gradually as out of a misted morning, without morbid curiosity or shock. The Indians understood the pattern of development that the young male follows, whether colt, young buffalo, or boy. First the unsteady legs struggled after the mother, then the young were gradually drawn together, until the males began to show a preference for their own kind. So the pre-puberty Indian boys raced and hunted in troops, in gangs, explored and played war together. In the old days the fathers and the holy men watched these boys, planning the time for the puberty fastings and rites. The warrior societies looked them over for prospective recruits, as did the relatives of young girls, the girls before whom the boys would soon be showing off, as the young Indian does now around the dances, the little pole corrals where the wild reservation horses are ridden, or in sports. Remnants of the old-time warrior societies, with their stress upon courage, fortitude, a straight tongue, and responsibility for the peace and the protection of the people still survive. Some of these ideals are carrying over into the Indian version of such groups as the 4-H Clubs and the Boy Scouts. A young Cheyenne who wrote me from Korea that he spent his eighteenth birthday in a foxhole had some of his preparation from the last of the Dog Soldier society, whose duty was never to leave a position until the last straggler of the village was safely away, and thereby won themselves the reputation as the most stubborn and reckless fighters of the Plains.

Even with all the precautions, an occasional youth failed to make his way to complete maturity; perhaps through some early sickness or injury he never quite got away from his mother's moccasin tracks into manhood. He, like all members of Indian society somehow set apart, as the blind, the crippled, or those whose medicine dreams forbade killing, was looked upon as possessing some special gift for the preservation of the people. He was considered of special sensitivity, particularly outside of the realm of fact and reality, and so became an agency intriguer, as he once would have been a spy and a diviner of future encounters with the enemy, particularly for formal war parties going into battle. Sometimes a black hood to cover all the head was part of his diviner's regalia, designed to isolate him from all sight and sound, to complete his release from actuality.

Normally the young Indian's attitude toward girls was established early. "See how the boy is with the women of his lodge and you can know how the young man will be with your daughter—" was an old saying among the Cheyennes, where virtue in a woman was most highly prized. Overfamiliarity has been discouraged since the days in the skin lodges, when perhaps seven or more lived about a winter fire, and father in the place of honor at the back, the youths and boys to his left, the women and girls to the right, with an old woman at the lodge opening as keeper of the entrance, seeing all who came and went. Such close living demanded an iron paternal hand, unknown among these Indians, or a well-established pattern of conduct if there was to be order and peace all those confining months.

From about his seventh year a boy stopped addressing his sisters and his adopted sisters directly, speaking to them only through a third person, even in the persistent joking of the Sioux.

"Fat Boy seems to like watching the sun go down over our pigpen," I once heard a young Indian say, as though to the mouth harp he was pounding against his knee. His pretty sister did not reply but went about her supper preparations. She could not have defended her plumpish suitor any more than she would have noticed him those first few times that he stopped his old car as though only to smoke a cigarette with the men folks in the yard. "Our spotted colt will make a good one for the rodeos," she said. "He has already thrown the big rider of our family—" not looking at the skinned face of her brother, but laughing softly.

Something of even the stricter formalities has survived.

The Indian boy also sees the religion of his people all about him from the date of his birth. The older, more important men of his family probably still offer the first puff of the council pipe, the first bite of food each meal, to the sky, the earth, and the four great directions, which together are the Great Powers in whom every man, every creature, every rock and cloud and tree are united in brotherhood. In such a philosophy hatred can never be honestly harbored, not even hatred of an enemy. During the protracted if sporadic intertribal conflicts of the buffalo days, war prisoners sometimes became wives of head chiefs and returned to visit their people with their husbands. Captured men and boys too might be taken into the tribe. Sitting Bull's adopted brother was a war captive and honored all his lifetime by the Sioux. Imagine the alarm if our President adopted a young Communist war prisoner as his brother, brought him to live at the White House, had him at his elbow in all the councils of strategy as Sitting Bull did.

The Indians have added much of this concept and the rituals of the Great Powers to their notion of Christian beliefs and symbols, and with the peyote trances from the southwest, have formed the Native American Church, which, judged good or bad, is their own. But even those who joined the churches of the white man have clung to some of their basic beliefs. One Sunday morning, while camped along an agency trail, I went out for wash water from the creek. As I stooped to dip it up, I heard low Indian singing and the swish of water below me. A young Sioux knelt among the gray-green willows of the bank washing a blue shirt. He lifted it high from the water towards the sky and then dipped it towards the earth and all around, as the pipe and food are offered. Silently I slipped away, and a couple of hours later the young man came riding by, wearing the clean blue shirt. He raised his hand in greeting, palm out, in the old, old gesture of friendship, the left hand because it is nearest the heart and has shed no man's blood. He was on his way to Mass at the Mission, where his father and grandfather had joined when they came in from the buffalo ranges—going in a shirt offered in the old way to the Powers of the world, and the recognition of his brotherhood in them.

The realization of death too comes early and naturally to the young Sioux and Cheyenne. There was no demonology among these peoples, no evil being or spirit to be appeased or circumvented. If things did not go well it was not due to supernatural anger but because the people and their leaders were out of tune with the Great Powers. To discover what must be done men went to fast on high places, hoping for guidance in their dreaming, or endured mutilating humiliation of the flesh to bring a higher sensitivity to the spirit, a greater discernment and understanding and humility.

These Indians still do not take Satan and hell-fire very seriously, or the concept of an avenging God. The whole idea of building up fear is very alien to their philosophy, their ideal of personal discipline, their notion of the good life, and their conception of death. There was no fear of the dead and no uneasiness about them. The body of a warrior who fell in enemy country was rescued immediately if possible, or by a later party sent out with the skin sack painted red for the honorable return. Often relatives and friends went to sit at a burial scaffold, now the cemetery, as they would have gone to the fireside of the departed one. Children saw the sickness, the dying, the burial, and often went along to visit the burial place and listen to the story of the duties and responsibilities left behind. Sometimes there was a song or two, or a few ceremonial dance steps. Once, on my way home with a bundle of wood, I ran into an old Indian dancing gravely by himself on a little knoll. The man was a stranger but curiosity drew me closer and closer, and when he noticed me I started to run, guilty because I had spied on a grownup.

But the old Indian called me back with the one word, "Granddaughter—" Gravely, with pictures in the dust and his sign talk, which I understood very imperfectly, he told me the story of the old woman who lived in the moon that was just rising full out of the east. He showed me the burden of wood she had hurriedly gathered before the storm that always followed the moon's first waning. Then he talked of other things, why he had come here, where over fifty years ago a great man of his people had been left on a scaffold, to return to the grass that fed the buffalo, who would, in his turn, feed the Indian.

I left the man there, filling his feathered stone pipe, the last of the evening sun on his wrinkled face and his neat, fur-wrapped braids. He was a scarred old warrior come to the burial place of a chief killed by white soldiers. Yet he could call a barefoot child of these whites, a stranger, "granddaughter," and tell her a story to dignify the detested task of wood bearing.

This Indian use of the words *grandson* and *granddaughter* contains, I think, the essence of their attitude towards the young. The first lesson of the new-born child teaches him that in matters of public safety, public good, the individual must subordinate himself to the group. But in return he senses from the first that all his community has an equal responsibility towards him. Every fire will welcome him, every pot will have a little extra for a hungry boy, and every ear is open to his griefs, his joys, and aspirations. And as his world expands he finds himself growing with it, into a society that needs no locks against him, no paper to record his word, and no threat of ostracism. He is a free man because he has learned to discipline himself, and a happy one because he can discharge his duties and responsibilities to others and to himself as an oriented, an intrinsic part of his community, a partner in a wide, encompassing brother-hood.

The Christmas of the Phonograph Records

It seems to me that I remember it all quite clearly. The night was very cold, footsteps squeaking in the frozen snow that had lain on for over two weeks, the roads in our region practically unbroken. But now the holidays were coming and wagons had pushed out on the long miles to the railroad, with men enough to scoop a trail for each other through the deeper drifts.

My small brother and I had been asleep in our attic bed long enough to frost the cover of the feather tick at our faces when there was a shouting in the road before the house, running steps, and then the sound of the broom handle thumping against the ceiling below us, and Father booming out, "Get up! The phonograph is here!"

The phonograph! I stepped out on the coyote skin at our bed, jerked on my woolen stockings and my shoes, buttoning my dress as I slipped down the outside stairs in the fading moon. Lamplight was pouring from the open door in a cloud of freezing mist over the back end of a loaded wagon, with three neighbors easing great boxes off, Father limping back and forth shouting, "Don't break me my records!" his breath white around his dark beard.

Inside the house Mother was poking sticks of wood into

the firebox of the cookstove, her eyes meeting mine for a moment, shining, her concern about the extravagance of a talking machine when we needed overshoes for our chilblains apparently forgotten. The three largest boxes were edged through the doorway and filled much of the kitchen–living room floor. The neighbors stomped their felt boots at the stove and held their hands over the hot lids while Father ripped at the boxes with his crowbar, the frozen nails squealing as they let go. First there was the machine, varnished oak, with a shining cylinder for the records, and then the horn, a great black, gilt-ribbed morning glory, and the crazy angled rod arm and chain to hold it in place.

By now a wagon full of young people from the Dutch community on Mirage Flats turned into our yard. At a school program they had heard about the Edison phonograph going out to Old Jules Sandoz. They trooped in at our door, piled their wraps in the leanto and settled along the benches to wait.

Young Jule and James, the brothers next to me in age, were up too, and watching Father throw excelsior aside, exposing a tight packing of round paper containers a little smaller than a middle-sized baking powder can, with more layers under these, and still more below. Father opened one and while I read out the instructions in my German-accented fifth-grade country school English, he slipped the brown wax cylinder on the machine, cranked the handle carefully, and set the needle down. Everybody waited, leaning forward. There was a rhythmic frying in the silence, and then a whispering of sound, soft and very, very far away.

It brought a murmur of disappointment and an escaping laugh, but gradually the whispers loudened into the sextet from *Lucia*, into what still seems to me the most beautiful singing in the world. We all clustered around, the visitors, fourteen, fifteen by now, and Mother too, caught while pouring hot chocolate into cups, her long-handled pan still tilted in the air. Looking back I realize something of the meaning of the light in her face: the hunger for music she must have felt, coming from Switzerland, the country of music, to a western Nebraska government claim. True, we sang old country songs in the evenings, she leading, teaching us all she knew, but plainly it had not been enough, really nothing.

By now almost everybody pushed up to the boxes to see what there was to play, or called out some title hopefully. My place in this was established from the start. I was to run the machine, play the two-minute records set before me. There were violin pieces for Father, among them *Alpine Violets* and *Mocking Bird* from the first box opened; *Any Rags, Red Wing*, and *I'm Trying so Hard to Forget You* for the young people; *Rabbit Hash* for my brothers, their own selection from the catalog; and Schubert's *Serenade* and *Die Kapelle* for Mother, with almost everyone laughing over *Casey at the Telephone*, all except Father. He claimed he could not understand such broken English, he who gave even the rankest westernism a French pronunciation.

With the trail broken to the main bridge of the region, just below our house, and this Christmas Eve, there was considerable travel on the road, people passing most of the night. The lighted windows, the music, the gathering of teams and saddlehorses in the yard, and the sub-zero weather tolled them in to the weathered little frame house with its leanto.

"You better set more yeast. We will have to bake again tomorrow," Mother told me as she cut into a *zopf*, one of the braids of coffee cake baked in tins as large as the circle of both her arms. This was the last of five planned to carry us into the middle of holiday week.

By now the phonograph had been moved to the top of the washstand in our parents' kalsomined bedroom, people sitting on the two double beds, on the round-topped trunk and on benches carried in, some squatting on their heels along the wall. The little round boxes stood everywhere, on the dresser and on the board laid from there to the washstand and on the window sills, with more brought in to be played and Father still shouting over the music, "Don't break me my records!" Some were broken, the boxes slipping out of unaccustomed or cold-stiffened hands, the brown wax perhaps already cracked by the railroad.

When the Edison Military Band started a gay, blaring galop, Mother looked in at the bedroom door, pleased. Then she noticed all the records spread out there, and in the kitchen-living room behind her, and began to realize their number. "Three hundred!" she exclaimed in German, speaking angrily in Father's direction, "Looks to me like more than three thousand!"

Father scratched under his bearded chin, laughing slyly. "I added to the order," he admitted. He didn't say how many, nor that there were other brands besides the Edison here, including several hundred foreign recordings obtained through a Swiss friend in New York, at a stiff price.

Mother looked at him, her blue eyes tragic, as she could make them. "You paid nothing on the mortgage! All the twenty-one-hundred-dollar inheritance wasted on a talking machine!"

No, Father denied, puffing at his corncob pipe. Not all. But Mother knew him well. "You did not buy the overshoes for the children. You forgot everything except your stamp collection, your guns, and the phonograph!"

"The overshoes are coming. I got them cheaper on time, with the guns."

"More debts!" she accused bitterly, but before she could add to this one of the young Swiss, Maier perhaps, or Paul Freye, grabbed her and, against the stubbornness of her feet, whirled her back into the kitchen in the galop from the Edison band. He raced Mother from door to stove and back again and around and around, so her blue calico skirts flew out and the anger died from her face. Her eyes began to shine in an excitement I had never seen in them, and I realize now, looking back, all the fun our mother missed in her working life, even in her childhood in the old country, and during the much harder years later.

That galop started the dancing. Hastily the table was pushed against the wall, boxes piled on top of it, the big ones dragged into the leanto. Waltzes, two-steps, quadrilles, and schottisches were sorted out and set in a row ready for me to play while one of the men shaved a candle over the kitchen floor. There was room for only one set of square dancers but our bachelor neighbor, Charley Sears, called the turns with enthusiasm. The Peters girls, two school teachers, and several other young women whom I've forgotten were well outnumbered by the men, as is common in new communities. They waltzed, two-stepped, formed a double line for a Bohemian polka, or schottisched around the room, one couple close behind the other to, perhaps, *It Blew, Blew, Blew*. Once Charley Sears grabbed my hand and drew me out to try a quadrille, towering over me as he swung me on the corner and guided me through the allemande left. My heart pounded in shyness and my home-made shoes compounded my awkwardness. Later someone else dragged me out into a two-step, saying, "Like this: 'one, two; one, two.' Just let yourself go."

Ah, so that was how it was done. Here started a sort of craze that was to hold me for over twenty years, through the bear dance, the turkey trot, the Charleston, and into the Lindy hop. But that first night with the records even Old Jules had to try a round polka, even with his foot crippled in a long-ago well accident. When he took his pipe out of his mouth, dropped it lighted into his pocket, and whirled Mother around several times we knew that this was a special occasion. Before this we had never seen him even put an arm around her.

After the boys had heard their selection again, and *The Preacher and the Bear*, they fell asleep on the floor and were carried to their bed in the leanto. Suddenly I remembered little Fritzlie alone in the attic, perhaps half-frozen. I hurried up the slippery, frosted steps. He was crying, huddled together under the feather tick, cold and afraid, deserted by the cat too, sleeping against the warm chimney. I brought the boy down, heavy hulk that he was, and laid him in with his brothers. By then the last people started to talk of leaving, but the moon had clouded over, the night-dark roads winding and treacherous through the drifts. Still, those who had been to town must get home with the Christmas supplies and such presents as they could manage for their children when they awoke in the morning.

Toward dawn Father dug out *Sempach*, a song of a heroic Swiss battle, in which one of Mother's ancestors fell, and *Andreas Hofer*, of another national hero. Hiding her pleasure at these records, Mother hurried away to the cellar under the house for two big hams, one to boil while the Canada goose roasted for the Christmas dinner. From the second ham she sliced great red rounds for the frying pan and I mixed up a triple batch of baking powder biscuits and set on the two-gallon coffee pot. When the sun glistened on the frosted snow, the last of the horses huddled together in our yard were on the road. By then some freighters forced to camp out by an upset wagon came whipping their teams up the icy pitch from the Niobrara River and stopped in. Father was slumped in his chair, letting his pipe fall into his beard, but he looked up and recognized the men as from a ranch accused of driving out bona fide settlers. Instead of rising to order them off the place he merely said "How!" in the Plains greeting, and dropped back into his doze. Whenever the music stopped noticeably, he lifted his shaggy head, complaining, "Can't you keep the machine going?" even if I had my hands in the biscuits. "Play the *Mocking Bird* again," he might order, or a couple of the expensive French records of pieces he had learned to play indifferently in the violin lessons of his boyhood in Neuchatel. He liked *Spring Song* too, and *La Paloma*, an excellent mandolin rendition of *Come ye Disconsolate*, and several German love songs he had learned from his sweetheart, in Zurich, who had not followed him to America.

Soon my three brothers were up again and calling for their favorites as they settled to plates of ham with red gravy and biscuits, Fritzlie from the top of two catalogs piled on a chair shouting too, just to be heard. None of them missed the presents that we never expected on Christmas; besides, what could be finer than the phonograph?

While Mother fed our few cattle and the hogs I worked at the big stack of dishes with one of the freighters to wipe them. Afterward I got away to the attic and slept a little, the music from below faint through my floating of dreams. Suddenly I awoke, remembering what day this was and that young Jule and I had hoped Father might go cottontail hunting in the canyons up the river and help us drag home a little pine tree. Christmas had become a time for a tree, even without presents, a tree and singing, with at least one new song learned.

I dressed and hurried down. Father was asleep and there were new people in the bedroom and in the kitchen too, talking about the wonder of the music rolling steadily from the big horn. In our Swiss way we had prepared for the usual visitors during the holidays, with family friends on Christmas and surely some of the European homeseekers Father had settled on free land, as well as passers by just dropping in to get warm and perhaps be offered a cup of coffee or chocolate or a glass of Father's homemade wine if particularly privileged. Early in the forenoon the Syrian peddler we called Solomon drew up in the yard with his high four-horse wagon. I remember him every time I see a picture of Krishna Menon—the tufted hair, the same lean yellowish face and long white teeth. Solomon liked to strike our place for Christmas because there might be customers around and besides there was no display of religion to make him uncomfortable in his Mohammedanism, Father said, although one might run into a stamp-collecting priest or a hungry preacher at our house almost any other time.

So far as I know, Solomon was the first to express what others must have thought. "Excuse it please, Mrs. Sandoz," he said, in the polite way of peddlers, "but it seem to un-educated man like me the new music is for fine palace—"

Father heard him. "Nothing's too good for my family and my neighbors," he roared out.

"The children have the frozen feet—" the man said quietly.

"Frozen feet heal! What you put in the mind lasts!"

The peddler looked down into his coffee cup, half full of sugar, and said no more.

It was true that we had always been money poor and plainly would go on so, but there was plenty of meat and game, plenty of everything that the garden, the young orchard, the field, and the open country could provide, and for all of which there was no available market. Our bread, dark and heavy, was from our hard macaroni wheat ground at a local water mill. The hams, sausage, and bacon were from our own smokehouse, the cellar full of our own potatoes, barrels of pickles and sauerkraut, and hundreds of jars of canned fruit and vegetables, crocks of jams and jellies, wild and tame, including buffalo berry, that wonderful, tart, golden-red jelly from the silvery bush that seems to retreat before close settlement much like the buffalo and the whooping crane. Most of the root crops were in a long pit outside, and the attic was strung with little sacks of herbs and poppy seed, bigger ones of dried green beans, sweetcorn, chokecherries, sandcherries, and wild plums. Piled along the low sides of the attic were bushel bags of popcorn, peas, beans, and lentils, the flour stacked in rows with room between for the mousing cat.

Sugar, coffee, and chocolate were practically all we bought for the table, with perhaps a barrel of blackstrap molasses for cookies and brown cake, all laid in while the fall roads were still open.

When the new batch of coffee cake was done and the fresh bread and buns, the goose in the oven, we took turns getting scrubbed at the heater in the leanto, and put on our best clothes, mostly made-over from some adult's but well-sewn. Finally we spread Mother's two old country linen cloths over the table lengthened out by boards laid on salt barrels for twenty-two places. While Mother passed the platters, I fed the phonograph with records that Mrs. Surber and her three musical daughters had selected, soothing music: Bach, Mozart, Brahms, and the *Moonlight Sonata* on two foreign records that Father had hidden away so they would not be broken, along with an a capella *Stille Nacht* and some other foreign ones Mother wanted saved. For lightness, Mrs. Surber had added *The Last Rose of Summer*, to please Elsa, the young soprano soon to be a professional singer in Cleveland, and a little Strauss and Puccini, while the young people wanted Ada Jones and *Monkey Land* by Collins and Harlan.

There was stuffed Canada goose with the buffalo berry jelly; ham boiled in a big kettle in the leanto; watercress salad; chow-chow and pickles, sweet and sour; dried green beans cooked with bacon and a hint of garlic; carrots, turnips, mashed potatoes and gravy, with coffee from the start to the pie, pumpkin and gooseberry. At the dishpan set on the high water bench, where I had to stand on a little box for comfort, the dishes were washed as fast as they came off the table, with a relay of wipers. There were also waiting young men and boys to draw water from the bucket well, to chop stove wood and carry it in.

As I recall now, there were people at the table for hours. A letter of Mother's says that the later uninvited guests got sausage and sauerkraut, squash, potatoes, and fresh bread, with canned plums and cookies for dessert. Still later there was a big roaster full of beans and sidemeat brought in by a lady homesteader, and some mince pies made with wild plums to lend tartness instead of apples, which cost money.

All this time there was the steady stream of music and talk from the bedroom. I managed to slip in the *Lucia* a couple of times until a tart-tongued woman from over east said she believed I was getting addled from all that hollering. We were not allowed to talk back to adults, so I put on the next record set before me, this one *Don't Get Married Any More, Ma*, selected for a visiting Chicago widow looking for her fourth husband, or perhaps her fifth. Mother rolled her eyes up at this bad taste, but Father and the other old timers laughed over their pipes.

We finally got Mother off to bed in the attic for her first nap since the records came. Downstairs the floor was cleared and the Surber girls showed their dancing-school elegance in the waltzes. There was a stream of young people later in the afternoon, many from the skating party at the bridge. Father, red-eyed like the rest of us, limped among them, soaking up their praise, their new respect. By this time my brothers and I had given up having a tree. Then a big boy from up the river rode into the yard dragging a pine behind his horse. It was a shapely tree, and small enough to fit on a box in the window, out of the way. The youth was the son of Father's worst enemy, the man who had sworn in court that Jules Sandoz shot at him, and got our father thirty days in jail, although everybody, including the judge, knew that Jules Sandoz was a crack shot and what he fired at made no further appearances.

As the son came in with the tree, someone announced loudly who he was. I saw Father look toward his Winchester on the wall, but he was not the man to quarrel with an enemy's children. Then he was told that the boy's father himself was in the yard. Now Jules Sandoz paled above his bearding, paled so the dancers stopped, the room silent under the suddenly foolish noise of the big-horned machine. Helpless, I watched Father jump toward the rifle. Then he turned, looked to the man's gaunt-faced young son.

"Tell your old man to come in. We got some good Austrian music."

So the man came in, and sat hunched over near the door. Father had left the room, gone to the leanto, but after a while he came out, said his "How!" to the man, and paid no attention when Mrs. Surber pushed me forward to make the proper thanks for the tree that we were starting to trim as usual. We played *The Blue Danube* and some other pieces long forgotten now for the man, and passed him the coffee and *küchli* with the others. He tasted the thin flaky frycakes. "Your mother is a good cook," he told me. "A fine woman."

When he left with the skaters all of Father's friends began to talk at once, fast, relieved. "You could have shot him down, on your own place, and not got a day in the pen for it," one said.

Old Jules nodded. "I got no use for his whole outfit, but the music is for everybody."

As I recall now, perhaps half a dozen of us, all children,

worked at the tree, looping my strings of red rose hips and popcorn around it, hanging the people and animal cookies with chokecherry eyes, distributing the few Christmas tree balls and the tinsel and candleholders that the Surbers had given us several years before. I brought out the boxes of candles I had made by dipping string in melted tallow, and then we lit the candles and with my schoolmates I ran out into the cold of the road to look. The tree showed fine through the glass.

Now I had to go to bed, although the room below me was alive with dancing and I remembered that Jule and I had not sung our new song, *Amerika ist ein schönes Land* at the tree.

Holiday week was much like Christmas, the house full of visitors as the news of the fine music and the funny records spread. People appeared from fifty, sixty miles away and farther so long as the new snow held off, for there was no other such collection of records in all of western Nebraska, and none with such an open door. There was something for everybody, Irishmen, Scots, Swedes, Danes, Poles, Czechs as well as the Germans and the rest, something pleasant and nostalgic. The greatest variety in tastes was among the Americans, from *Everybody Works but Father*, *Arkansas Traveler*, and *Finkelstein at the Seashore* to love songs and the sentimental *Always in the Way;* from home and native region pieces to the patriotic and religious. They had strong dislikes too, even in war songs. One settler, a GAR veteran, burst into tears and fled from the house at the first notes of *Tenting Tonight*. Perhaps it was the memories it awakened. Many Americans were as interested in classical music as any European, and it wasn't always a matter of cultivated taste. One illiterate little woman from down the river cried with joy at Rubinstein's *Melody in F.*

"I has heard me talkin' and singin' before," she said apologetically as she wiped her eyes, "but I wasn't knowin' there could be something sweet as that come from a horn."

Afternoons and evenings, however, were still the time for the dancers. Finally it was New Year, the day when the Sandoz relatives, siblings, uncles and cousins, gathered, perhaps twenty of them immigrants brought in by the land locator, Jules. This year they were only a sort of eddy in the regular stream of outsiders. Instead of nostalgic jokes and talk of the family and the old country, there were the records to hear, particularly the foreign ones, and the melodies of the old violin lessons that the brothers had taken, and the guitar and mandolin of their one sister. Jules had to endure a certain amount of joking over the way he spent most of his inheritance. One brother was building a cement block home in place of his soddy with his, and a greenhouse. The sister was to have a fine large barn instead of a new home because her husband believed that next year Halley's comet would bring the end of the world. Ferdinand, the youngest of the brothers, had put his money into wild-cat oil stock and planned to become very wealthy.

Although most of their talk was in French, which Mother did not speak, they tried to make up for this by complimenting her on the excellence of her chocolate and her golden fruit cake. Then they were gone, hot bricks at their feet, and calling back their adieus from the freezing night. It was a good thing they left early, Mother told me. She had used up the last of the chocolate, the last cake of the twenty-five pound caddies. We had baked up two sacks of flour, forty-nine pounds each, in addition to all that went into the Christmas preparations before the phonograph came. Three-quarters of a hundred pound bag of coffee had been roasted, ground, and used during the week, and all the winter's sausage and ham. The floor of the kitchen–living room, old and worn anyway, was much thinner for the week of dancing. New Year's night a man who had been there every day, all week, tilted back on one of the kitchen chairs and went clear through the floor.

"Oh, the fools!" Father shouted at us all. "Had to wear out my floor dancing!"

But plainly he was pleased. It was a fine story to tell for years, all the story of the phonograph records. He was particularly gratified by the praise of those who knew something about music, people like the Surbers and a visitor from a Czech community, a relative of Dvorak, the great composer. The man wrote an item for the papers, saying, "This Jules Sandoz has not only settled a good community of homeseekers, but is enriching their cultural life with the greatest music of the world."

"Probably wants to borrow money from you," Mother said. "He has come to the wrong door."

Gradually the records for special occasions and people were stored in the leanto. For those used regularly, Father and a neighbor made a lot of flat boxes to fit under the beds, always handy, and a cabinet for the corner at the bedroom door. The best, the finest from both the Edison and the foreign recordings, were put into this cabinet, with a door that didn't stay closed. One warmish day when I was left alone with the smaller children, the water pail needed re-filling. I ran out to draw a bucket from the well. It was a hard and heavy pull for a growing girl and I hated it, always afraid that I wouldn't last, and would have to let the rope slip and break the windlass.

Somehow, in my uneasy hurry, I left the door ajar. The wind blew it back and when I had the bucket started up the sixty-five foot well, our big old sow, loose in the yard, pushed her way into the house. Horrified, I shouted to

Fritzlie to get out of her way, but I had to keep pulling and puffing until the bucket was at the top. Then I ran in. Fritzlie was up on a chair, safe, but the sow had knocked down the record cabinet and scattered the cylinders over the floor. Standing among them as in corn, she was chomping down the wax records that had rolled out of the boxes, eating some, box and all. Furiously I thrashed her out with the broom, amidst squealings and shouts. Then I tried to save what I could. The sow had broken at least thirty or thirty-five of the best records and eaten all or part of twenty more. *La Paloma* was gone, and *Traumerei* and *Spring Song; Evening Star* too, and half of the *Moonlight Sonata* and many others, foreign and domestic, including all of Brahms.

I got the worst whipping of my life for my carelessness, but the loss of the records hurt more, and much, much longer.

The Neighbor

Charley Sears came to our region, the upper Niobrara River country, sometime in the 1880's as a youth with his landseeking family. Later he bought a small place one mile east of us. Another Irishman had owned it, until he marketed a good wheat crop and started home with the money in his pocket and a jug of whisky under the wagon seat for comfort on the lonely night road. Next day the team was found grazing beside the trail, Pat dead in the wagon box. He had fallen forward with his throat across the dashboard and choked to death. Before that, lightning had struck Pat's place a dozen times. Once it knocked out all four corners of his house and left him unconscious. The place was a hoodoo, a jinx, Pat said, and after he died some agreed.

But although Charley Sears knew a lot of fine ghost stories, he was not the man for such nonsense as jinxes and hoodoos. Perhaps it was his sensible Scotch-Irish ancestry coming out and whatever infusions were picked up in the migration from early Pennsylvania through Kentucky to western Nebraska. Although I was a small girl then, I recall when he moved in. One afternoon a big wagon drew ponderously up the sandy pitch from the Niobrara River —a bundle rack loaded with beds, dresser, kitchen stove, cupboards, and other household goods. The three, four milk cows plodding behind the wagon were driven by a horsebacker, a fine straight figure in the saddle. I watched as I often did along our road, crouched down in the green forest of our asparagus patch where I could see the travelers headed toward the free-land region east of us: freighters, cowboys, occasional herds of cattle and sheep trailing in from Wyoming, and always the homeseekers from far places.

When the horsebacker with his cows seemed well past, I stood up, hanging to the baby brother astride my hip, but the man must have seen me as he rode by for he turned in the saddle, lifted a hand in the western greeting, and smiled to me. It was an amused smile for a peaked-faced, spying little girl, and more friendly than from the ranch hands, more restrained than from the usual settlers—probably men that my father had located on new homes. I was desperately shy and withdrawn then, and so, embarrassed and ashamed, I dropped back down into the feathery green of the asparagus. The sharp dusty smell comes back to me now, and the warmth and friendliness of the man, perhaps because I met that same greeting, those same teasing, smiling eyes several times a week for most of the remaining years of my childhood.

It was some time before I discovered that this man was Charley Sears, our new neighbor, or noticed him any more than a child would where people drift through like tumbleweeds on the vagrant wind. Besides, there was the antagonism left for Pat, his dead predecessor, with whom my father had sustained a rifle-carrying feud that naturally never came to any actual shooting, and had certainly terrified Pat considerably less than it had me.

Although Charley Sears took no sides in the quarrels common to a new region, and those sprouted by my father's need for drama, he was soon established as our good neighbor. Like many new settlers, he was a bachelor but not a bunch quitter, no loner. If necessary Charley could fiddle and call a good square-dance set. He was willing and handy at branding, butchering, threshing, house or barn raising, and in time of flood or prairie fire. He sat up with the sick and the dead and knew how to comfort the sorrowful, the alarmed. He had helped gather the settlers to the sod blockhouse on his uncle's place back in the Ghost Dance Indian scare, and had ridden out of its protection to find a lost puppy that one of the children cried for at night.

Charley had known my father, Jules Sandoz, in the early days and understood something of this Swiss visionary who had the patience to develop an orchard where no tame fruit had ever grown, and who was crippled for life through a practical joke that exploited his extreme excitability. Charley had seen Old Jules work to protect the early settlers, and when the new courts wouldn't act against a man who was burning them out, one after the other, and shooting at the women through the windows, the youth Charley Sears joined the vigilante group my father raised. He was along when they hanged the pyromaniac but with incredible good luck were saved from murder by the toughness of the man's neck. They let him down, and he had them all arrested.

After that there had been little contact between Old Jules and the Sears family. They had their own problems, but they managed to stay on through the nineties when drouth and hard times shook loose many settlers with hardier taproots. Charley knew that Father had been arrested several times for apparently shooting at his neighbors, and also that he would go to his worst enemy in a blizzard to deliver a new baby. Everybody knew he would be out on a hill looking if one of his children was a few minutes late coming home, and limping anxiously up and down if one of them had even a trifling fever, but he whipped one of them at six weeks until his arm was weary and his anger spent because the infant cried in the night.

Without apparent uneasiness our new neighbor set up a mailbox next to ours on the daily route a mile west of us, and whoever went for the mail first brought it all as far as our place; so, one way or the other, we saw Charley almost every day. He could understand a lot of the German-Swiss dialect spoken in our house, and admired Mother's energetic efforts to keep her family fed and covered, while ignoring her cry of calamity at every turn, and her pride in telling everyone the baldest truth about himself.

The first night the new neighbor stopped by he spied me back in the shadows of the lamp with the sleeping baby across my knees. Afterward he took a remote but unfailing notice of me, not as an occasionally diligent child, a "good little mother," or "a little old grandmother," as I often heard myself described, or even as the child of a man who helped the landless. Charley showed an amused tolerance of me as myself despite my old-womanish ways and my curiously aged face that so often brought exclamations from strangers. Looking back, I can guess how disturbing we children must have been to such a thoughtful man, isolated as we were from anyone of our own age, speaking almost no English, and growing up in that immoderate, even volcanic household. I think Charley worked on me particularly, and perhaps properly, as the eldest. With Father crippled and an intellectual, most of the field and orchard work fell to Mother, and so most of the care of the other children was left to me. Because Father must never be disturbed into a temper by a crying baby again, each new one was put into my bed at around the third week and from then on was mine to feed and diaper and comfort, and to amuse as well as to teach.

From the first Charley Sears liked to tease me a little, but gently, about the two-headed shadow creature that followed me and the baby on my hip wherever I went. He entranced my brothers by making pennies disappear from their palms, to be found in their pockets or behind their ears. Once, after their cries of joy and my usual silence, although I had edged a bit closer, he looked over to me and demanded, "Cat got your tongue?" But his eyes were so gay and laughing that for once I didn't try to hide when made aware of myself. I did back away a little, but I recall that my brothers clung to the man's legs, begging for more tricks, begging him not to go home.

And once, after a rain, he surprised me while I was busily patting sand over my bare feet to make foot houses for my baby brother. We were laughing over them together when suddenly our neighbor was there on his horse, saying something about how this Miss Sobersides could giggle. I started to gather the baby up and run, but he leaned over and said, very softly, "You can't run away—" and suddenly I couldn't. After that he made many occasions for laughter, until he had to caution me now and then: "Little ladies don't show their gums when they laugh," saying it as he once said, "Ladies don't swing their arms, and they do their walking from below their hips."

Charley Sears was as straight as Father's Sioux friends, tall and well built, with gray-blue eyes and a dark bearding that was always clean shaven except for the moderate mustache. His brown hair lay in a lazy curl from the exceptionally neat part, a threading of gray creeping toward it from the temples. I recall thinking of him as around twenty-five, which seemed to me about the last stop before senility. Yet he must certainly have been older. The veining at his nose I knew came from a little steady dragging at the bottle although we never smelled more than a slight odor of spice about him, or found any change in his usual thoughtful, courteous way. He seldom drank publicly. In very cold weather he might have a bit with Father from the winter's bottle of Ilers Malt Whisky—barefoot as he called it, meaning neat.

Very early my mother let him know that winning my allegiance wasn't much of a conquest. She told him that by the time I was a year old I had been trailing after any man my short legs could keep in sight. Charley laughed, not to my mother but to me, and for the first time the story didn't seem a shameful and embarrassing thing.

Gradually this new neighbor drifted closer to our family, appearing Sundays at the edge of the casual, uninvited group that usually gathered at our place. He seldom stayed to dinner, although it couldn't have been because we were so hard up. It is true ours was a homegrown table, but a hearty one. "Plates enough to need the horse trough for the washing as 'tis," he might reply to Mother's invitation to stay for Sunday dinner. But usually his horse was tied to the fence again later in the afternoon, with Charley sitting at the wall somewhere, offering a complimentary word or two for the old country songs Mother started for us all while we washed the stacks of dishes, or perhaps while I peeled potatoes or picked wild ducks for the next meal.

Mother couldn't prevent bad language from Old Jules or even from herself in her moments of high emotion, but she would have none of it from us. Yet Charley Sears went a little farther than that with us. He protested that many of the first words of English we were learning were really slang or worse. He believed in poise and moderation in speech as well as in conduct. "All buzz and no barley," he would say when my impulsiveness or my temper carried me to silly extremes. He knew many amusing little poems that I learned later had morals tacked on—the kind of verses found in the public speakers of his youth. He taught some of them to me, laughing at my guttural German-Swiss pronunciation. He knew many folk songs and sometimes brought a yellowed old composition book to read me the words in faded pencil for, say, "The Gypsy Maiden," "Jimmy, Go Ile the Cairs," or "Mary across the Wild Moors" or songs he got from the Texas trail drivers on the ranches around us, "Red River," and "Streets of Laredo," and so on. Some he wouldn't read to me because they were not for a nice girl to know.

I remember that so very clearly now. Nobody had ever implied that I could possibly be a nice girl. Mother considered praise of her children as suspect as self-praise would be, and Father never spoke well of anyone who might make his words an excuse for less prompt jumping when he commanded. This included his wife and children, although later we discovered that he bragged on us all when far away, if he happened to recall our existence.

From the start Father said that Charley Sears had no get-up. He had come into the region early enough to get the cream of the free land and got not an acre of it. Even when he bought Pat's place he could have gone ten miles farther east and taken up a homestead free, much better land too, not the gravelly knobs that were a fine carpet of white and purple and magenta of loco bloom in summer, but with only a little strip of sandy farm ground. Perhaps Charley would have felt guilty doing his scratchy tilling on good earth. The house was a small story and a half set in a shallow pocket where lightning tended to strike, as even the unsuperstitious admitted. Perhaps there was a concentration of the rusty hematitic nodules common to our sandy deposits, enough of the iron to attract electricity, or, as some suggested, a deep dyke of wet earth reaching up through the dry. Anyway, horses, cattle, and the windmill had been destroyed in Pat's day, and the house struck repeatedly, in addition to the time the corners were blown out and Pat stretched out for dead—enough to drive any man to the jug. Of course the lightning kept right on striking there after Charley bought the place, but he put up rods, grounded his fences, and disconnected his telephone line at the first close roar of thunder.

Women often disliked homesteading far beyond the promise of school and neighbors, but bachelors usually didn't mind. Charley apparently liked close and noisy neighbors. His mother had been sickly and as a boy he learned to keep a spotless house for the family, his floor always white as sanded wood, his bread so fragrant it tolled the far traveler in off the prairie. Yet somehow he never made lesser housekeepers uncomfortable, although he used his Irish sayings now and then to inculcate a little tidiness into my housekeeping. "Where cobwebs grow, beaus don't go," he would say, but even at six I knew that when girls were scarce as in our region beaus went wherever they could.

We were five miles from the school in our district and Mother was too proud to have her children get out in public barefoot, whatever the distance. Father said American teachers were ignorant and that his children could learn more from him, which was possible. By my ninth year I had learned the multiplication table through the twenty-fives, understood such terms as *spiral nebulae* and *spontaneous generation* from Father's long discussions with visiting scientists. I could even write a passable hand in the old copy book that Charley Sears brought me, but nobody had bothered to show me that words were made of the alphabet, with some relation to the sounds of the letters, or that a certain word always looked the same. My inability to read disturbed our neighbor. Along in the summer he said that I must start to school in the fall. I answered in my broken English that it would not be permitted, and that I had not the shoes.

Charley laughed. "The shoes your mother will manage

as she does other things." Later it turned out that some-body reported my age to the county superintendent and my parents were compelled to send me and my brother Jules to school in the adjoining district, only three miles away. I was almost delirious with joy, and embarrassed that other children my age were at least in the third grade.

Charley Sears had usually been most careful not to go against the teachings of our parents, but as soon as I could read a little he ignored one of Father's pet notions. Fiction to Old Jules was for the hired man and hired girl, if you had them, but never for a Sandoz. Gradually Charley let me discover that he had something worth all the world to me then: a tall bookcase full of books, varying from Hawthorne, *Nicholas Nickleby*, and Bill Nye to Mary J. Holmes and *From Ballroom to Hell*. He also had a lot of old magazines, including at least ten years of a woman's periodical that left its sentimental mark on the attitudes and face and figure of a generation of village and country womanhood —*The Comfort*. Charley started to sneak these down for me, and because the attic where I slept with whoever was the baby had outside stairs, I could slip the books up to my bed and hide them in the straw tick. But even so there was never enough reading matter and I started to write stories for myself, very bad ones. Still, the first one was printed in the junior page of the Omaha *Daily News* and brought me a whipping and a short time in our cellar. As soon as Father's anger cooled he took me out quail hunting. Charley Sears approved of my writing but not of the product. "Still a tongue-tied Dutchman," he wrote on the margin of the story in the newspaper. Years later, when I sneaked away to take teachers' examination, Charley was a bit more encouraging. "Sticking feathers on a buzzard's neck won't make an eagle out of him," he told me, and then added, laughing, "but maybe you can fool 'em—"

Although I still had a baby on my hip at ten, a sister now, Mother began to think of my posture. " Walk straight as a princess even if your feet are dirty," she said. I tried, but I was very thin and small and there were, in addition to the baby, water to draw from the deep well, grain and flour to carry into the attic, and a hundred other heavy burdens that Mother was too busy or too tiny to manage. This, added to the stooped shoulders characteristic of Father's family, bent me round as a drawn Sioux bow. But Charley Sears brought a sawed-off broom-handle and showed me tricks with it. A substantial six-footer himself, he could grasp the stick with both hands, swing it back over his head, and crawl through it as smoothly as a garter snake going through a fence. I worked for months to do it as easily, and, for a time, became almost as straight as he. "Ah, ha!" Mother told him. " She still is tagging at a man's heels!" But for once she let me see she was pleased.

Long before this Charley had begun to work on my native tactlessness, emphasizing the need for special thought and gentleness. I could see that it worked for him. He was welcome anywhere in the region, particularly where there were young ladies. He always did his share to make the new schoolma'am welcome in the fall, paying her polite court until she was well acquainted and had a suitable beau. One of my teachers could have trapped this wily bachelor if she had been so minded. For a while I hoped there would be a piece of wedding cake for my pillow, to make me dream of my future beloved. But when I dared ask Charley about the wedding date, he was brusque and stiff. He wouldn't ask *me* such a personal ques-tion, ten, fifteen years from now, and embarrass me, he said. The next fall he was gallantly calling on another pretty teacher, but this time I tried to be tactful, although nobody else in my family ever worried about tact. Mother would say anything if she thought it would serve to set someone right. She generally felt it her duty to tell you that so-and-so was talking about you behind your back. She always told the truth, the last bitter drop of it.

"Carrying tar only dirties the hands," Charley once protested mildly to Mother, and I recalled a story told about him, about an early affair with a woman who still lived in the community and who still hinted that one of her sons was his. But this bit of tar not even Mother would ever carry to him.

By this time our father had bought a phonograph that we could not afford, and a lot of records; so there was music as well as good talk to draw visitors. Much as he liked our Irish records, Charley usually observed the custom of the West and didn't get off his horse if Father was away. But the night a burglar shot a lock of hair from my head, Charley came as soon as we got the cut telephone line repaired. Even then he brought a neighbor along, more for propriety than for help. If Father was home Charley generally settled somewhere against the wall in our smoky kitchen–living room, on a bench perhaps, or a box, listening. He usually took no part in Father's talk. Limited in education, he lacked the arrogance of the ignorant and was hungry for talk of ancient history, horticulture, the possible origins of the Niobrara River fossil beds, and so on. But he was gone the minute the talk turned to topics that aroused Father to his violent speeches on his injustices, real or fancied, or to complaints against the politicians, the mail service, cattlemen, or women. Somehow Charley was never pressed to side with Father in these tirades as almost anyone else would have been: that was Charley's tact, I suppose, tact and diplomacy.

Perhaps Charley Sears was really lonesome, a lonesome man even after his sister came to live with him. Perhaps he liked the occasional drink he got at our place, usually from a pitcher of wild-grape wine, with Mother's good smoked sausage and heavy bread of macaroni wheat set out on the cutting board. He was an accommodating old-time Westerner, to whom any request for help immediately became a cow in the well. He went to endless trouble to carry out errands in town for us, knowing that Old Jules' women folk didn't get to town even once a year. He let us hook a telephone to his little fence line, which was the top strand of the barbed-wire fence and efficient enough in dry weather, when no breachy animal had broken it down. Occasionally communication to the outside was possible through a very erratic central at the house of one of Father's enemies, but very useful in time of local calamity, say a prairie fire, mad-dog scare, or a child lost in a blizzard, although then the line was generally grounded by drifting snow. Charley let everybody know when bank robbers were fleeing our way, when an incapacitated settler's corn needed husking, or a shivaree was due. Not that any of us ever went to any social events. I had seldom spent two continuous hours away from home except at school.

Pioneer life is never free from emergencies very long and in our community the man who usually arrived first upon bad news was Charley Sears. He came the time my father's brother was shot by the hired killer of a ranch near by—shot down while milking a cow, right before his wife and seven children, and dying. Father was away in the sandhills, locating settlers in the cattle country and in much greater danger than his brother, or so it suddenly seemed to us. The sheriff was slow and the killer still loose.

That night was a very long one for us. Charley came down right after supper, as though for his mail, but calling out a loud greeting before he rode into the yard to let us know it wasn't the killer. He blinked in the lamp-lighted kitchen and sat down quietly but out of range of the windows, as Father always did in those dangerous years of cattleman-settler troubles. Several times during the evening men rode up looking for Old Jules to lead them against the ranch where the killer had worked, find him, drag him out to a telephone pole somewhere, burn the whole damn outfit to the ground. When Mother told them in her excited, melodramatic way that Father was away, off alone in the hills, they looked serious, perhaps even spoke darkly of bullets from behind some soapweed. While my brothers and I drew closer together in alarm, Charley remained quiet. "Jules will look out for himself," he said several times, perhaps remembering that Father was a crack shot, or thinking of the time he led the vigilantes to hang a tough-necked man, almost twenty years before.

Nobody except the babies went to bed. Young Jules and Jim stayed up near Charley while Mother tried to busy herself patching their worn overalls, but up at every sound, her faded blue eyes rolled dramatically toward me in a warning that this, *this* time it was the news of our uncle's death, or of Father's. Or perhaps the killer was at the door. Several times Charley went to look after his stomping horse and came back to tell more stories of squirrels and hornets' nests back in Kentucky, and of berryings and play parties, hoop snakes and sting tailers. He asked us riddles and casually pulled string tricks from his pockets; he made a dinner knife stand out straight from the edge of the table, got water up into an inverted glass without touching it, pulled matches from his pocket, and said, "Can you take two from twenty-two and leave only four?"

Midnight passed and the deep-toned old-country clock tocked the hours on. Once Mother's face was turned bleak as winter from the telephone. Men had ridden the sandhills since yesterday and now it was dawning and nobody had found any sign of Father or his wagon. Charley glanced from his coffee cup to the rounded stack of loaded guns always standing in the corner behind our door. "Nobody'll get close to Jules—they know it ain't healthy."

"But from far—"

Charley smiled, and looked to my concerned face and laid his matches out in five neat squares. "Remove three, and leave three whole squares," he said in the same teasing way that, eight hours earlier, he had said to my brothers, "Take a card—any card" from the spread deck he held out to them.

Somehow we lived through that time. Our uncle died, Father came home, and was ready in the doorway with his Winchester up when the killer rode around the corner of the house. No man worth his pay as range protection would go against a Winchester with a revolver, and from a faunching horse at that, but I can still see the white faces of my mother and brothers behind Father until the sneering man finally set his spurs and was gone.

It was years before I realized what that tragic time, particularly the night of waiting, after Uncle Emile was shot, might have meant to us without Charley Sears. Who can measure the effect it might have had on us children if there had been only the high-pitched lamentations of our singularly courageous but singularly excitable mother and the dark-faced, armed men riding in with their short, violent words, their warnings of the killer's probable coming? Not a tear was shed all that night, although Charley's eyes seemed to water a little as he swung into his saddle in the morning sunlight and looked down upon the barefoot little girl holding out a jar of plum jelly from the cellar.

Then there was the time my father was bitten by the rattlesnake. We got him home by sundown, nine, ten hours later. There the horses dropped in exhaustion in the harness, and once more our telephone was dead.

"Run for the doctor!" Mother cried, and helped lift Father from the buggy.

I ran for Charley Sears, a mile away, mostly uphill. Afterward I realized I could have run to a couple of other places, nearer, and with direct telephone line to a doctor, but I had let my feet lead me.

Soon after this we moved into the sandhills, and we seldom saw Charley any more. Three, four times he wrote me stiff, formal little letters, but evoking all the sense of wholeness and well-being many of us felt when around him, reawakening the affection and trust and respect that must have been planted that day he first rode past a little girl with a baby on her hip. Charley lived to be an old man, and when he died a clipping of his funeral was sent to me in New York. Suddenly I was confronted by a deep and disturbing loss. This man had tried to lead a peaked-faced, shy, and ashamed little girl down on the Niobrara to see that she could learn to be a person in her own right, a person outside of the comfort and security she might be for her small siblings. He made her see that perhaps she could live without too much embarrassment and shame over her shortcomings, no matter how barefooted she might have to remain. Perhaps she could learn to use a little of the tireless energy, the bald out-spokenness of her mother and yet restrain the excitability, the gloom and fault-finding that were also her inheritance. He showed her that the swift, almost murderous temper of her father need not be uncontrolled in her, even while she nursed a little of Old Jules' fierce intellectual independence and any bit of his creative builder's vision that, with luck, he might have bred in her.

But perhaps most of all Charley Sears feared the sense of persecution that destroyed so much of my father's fine talent. "No use trying to blame things on other people," he once said to me at a time when I needed the reproof particularly. "If you got a bellyache it's you that's been eating the green apples."

But even that he said with the old teasing smile, this good neighbor of ours.

Martha of the Yellow Braids

The day Martha came the sun was warm as May on the midwinter drifts, and I ran most of the two miles home from school in my hurry to see her. I had never been around girls much. In a frontier community they are usually scarce; besides, my father was so often embroiled in some spectacular battle for human rights or perhaps sitting out his fines in jail—a background apparently not considered the best by the local mothers of growing girls. So my few playmates were boys, often Polish boys, perhaps because they didn't seem to mind that I was spindly as a rake handle, with my hair roached close to save Mother the combing time, and that I usually had a baby astride my hip. Besides, there were always my brothers.

But the winter I was going on ten Martha came. My father was a locator, and one of his Bohemian settlers brought his family to live with us until he could plow the spring earth for the sod needed to build his house. This was common enough, except that there had never been a girl near my age before. Now there was Martha, eleven, and all the things my mother always wanted me to be: plump, white-skinned, a good bread-baker, a young lady with nice young-lady manners. Martha had grown up in

town around her mother's series of boarding houses and
showed no deplorable tendency to sneak off for an hour's
fishing or sledding, particularly not with rude little Polaks,
as she immediately labeled my playmates. Disloyally I
tolerated this insult to my friends, for Martha was not only
what my mother wanted me to be but all that I wanted too.
She was a big girl, free of babies, and she had pale yellow
braids thick as pile-driver rope to hang below her knees
or to wind in a crown about her head above her garnet
earrings from Vienna.

There were other things about Martha that attracted
me: her father's teasing pinches at her tight, pink cheek,
her mother's goodnight kiss—incredible as a storybook
existence to me. But I still think it was the braids that made
me desert my Polanders; the pale yellow braids and
Martha's way of whispering secrets as she walked beside
me with an arm chummily around my shoulders, almost
as though we were two of the pretty young Hollanders
from over on the Flats, or maybe even American girls.

There must have been the usual difficulties in our family
that spring: snow, cold, cattle dying, bills unpaid, and
surely Father's temper and his affinity for trouble. Mother
must have been as impatient with him as always, and with
me too, for I was certainly even less skillful at my work
around the facile-handed Martha, and certainly no prettier
than before. But I remember nothing much of those three
months except a vague, cloudy sort of happiness in my
discovery that I could have a friend like the other girls in
school. There was the usual housework to be done, with
Father away hunting or locating settlers, and Mother busy
with the stock and the feeding, the fences to be repaired,
the trees to be planted before the leaves came. Martha and
I told each other stories as I did the cleaning and fed the
baby—not any of those I had written myself, printed in
the junior page of our daily paper. It wasn't that I didn't

trust her to keep the secret of my writing from my folks; I was ashamed of the stories. Although I usually dismissed fairy tales as plain lying, I even listened to them from Martha because I couldn't bear to see the hurt that would come into her blue eyes if I said so. And one night, after her mother allowed me to brush the long, yellow hair, I cried hours of envious tears—I who had surely put such childish things behind me long ago.

April came, with tight little clumps of Easter daisies on the greening hillsides, and finally the new sodhouse on the homestead was begun. When the swallows were back with us to skim the morning air, I stood in our yard and waved my baby sister's hand to Martha in the wagon that was taking her into the sandhills. Of course we wrote letters, long ones, every week; then shorter and not so often, for Martha's mother was down at the railroad some-where running another boarding place, and Martha kept house for her father. Her letters were less of childish stories and more about such things as washing greasy overalls, churning, or singing for the Sunday school that a walking sky pilot had organized among the settlers. By this time there was another baby coming to our house, and while I still got away for an hour now and then, Mother needed my help more and made as much fun of the Polish boys as Martha ever did. Finally one of my brothers and I were sent to the hills to live alone on Father's new homestead, only a few miles from Martha. But I had never been allowed to go visiting and so it didn't occur to me to walk over to see her. Months later, when Mother had moved down too, Martha came for some wolf poison. A coyote was getting her turkeys. By now her skirts were to her shoetops and her talk was all of woman things to Mother. When she got into a young bachelor's top buggy in our yard I knew that I had been left years behind.

Of course we were still friendly, and in a couple of years

I got my hair coaxed out into braids long enough to cross at the back. With pins in it and the hems of my faded calico dresses let down, I felt as old as anybody. By that time we had a school district organized, the teacher boarding at our house, and Father giving occasional dances in the barn. Martha came, usually with her folks, and while her mother talked about good matches for the girl, her father pulled the accordion for our dancing. Calmly, easily, Martha would put her hand on the arms of the older men, some at least twenty-five, while I stumbled around the floor with boys of my age, bickering with them about who was to lead, or perhaps talking about bronco busting or pulling a skunk from his winter hole with barbed wire. We were still known as the two good friends and sometimes Martha left the woman bench and came over to whisper giggling secrets into my ear about who was asking her to eat supper or perhaps warning me against this man or that one who had to be watched.

"He'll hold you so tight you can't breathe, if you permit him—" using grown-up words about grown-up things that I pretended to understand.

By the time I had hair enough to cover a rat I managed to have as many dances left over when daylight came as Martha, but still not with the same crowd, for hers were with bachelors who had homesteads, cookstoves, and bed-steads waiting for their wives, while mine were mostly with fuzzy-faced young ranch hands, outsiders visiting relatives in the hills, or Eastern schoolboys working in the hay camps. I was handy at picking up new steps and I had discovered that a ready foot and a glib tongue would do much to discount what I saw when I stood before the looking-glass of Mother's dresser.

"Ah, you are always wasting your time with those silly boys—" Martha would try to warn me, using words from her mother's mouth against me.

The spring she was sixteen Martha came over on her flea-bitten old mare instead of sitting easy in some red-wheeled buggy. She had news, and a ring on her finger. Of course the diamond was small, she admitted before I could say it, but the setting was white gold, very stylish. Very expensive too, and much better than a big stone in cheap, old-style yellow tiffany. By then I had learned some young-lady ways too, and so I pretended that I liked the ring, although I wouldn't have been interested in a diamond the size of a boulder set in a ring of platinum the size of a wagon tire, for I was secretly planning to be a schoolteacher and have fine clothes and many beaus for years and years, maybe even write some more of my stories, but for grownups. Although certainly no romantic, I wasn't prepared for Martha's further admission—that she had never seen the man. It was all right, though, she assured me. His people and hers were friends back in the old country, and he was known as a good provider, strong, healthy, and twenty-two, right in the prime of life. Evidently Martha wasn't satisfied with what I managed to say, for she told me crossly that she hadn't expected me to appreciate a good man, not with my nose in a book all the time and without the sense to see that a girl had to do the best she could for herself while she was young.

The wedding was a year later, in June. Martha's father took them up to Rushville to be married. Although I didn't get to go along, I was supposed to pretend that I was the bridesmaid for the dinner. Mother let me cut a dress from a bolt of eleven-cent organdy on the shelf of our country store. Even with a bertha, said to be softening, the unrelieved white was so unbecoming that I dyed an old scarf for a sash. It turned out a dirty lavender, the best I could do with Father's red and blue inks. If I could have found even a stub of indelible pencil, the sash would have been a pungent but vivid purple. I tried the dress on, and while I looked no worse than I had all my sixteen years, somehow it seemed much worse. I even wondered why I had never tried holding my breath long enough to die. Of course there was the wolf poison on the top shelf of the shop, but that was a little drastic.

For the wedding present Mother cut ten yards off the family bolt of white outing flannel, and tied it up with a red ribbon from one of the candy boxes the hay waddies brought me. I came near crying over this baby bundle, which I considered most insulting and suggestive. But no one was interested in my opinion, and, besides, I had to take something. Fortunately Father's peonies were particularly fine that year, and the only clumps in all the sandhills. He let me cut a whole armful, half of them deep wine-red and the rest white. I rolled these in a newspaper twist and tied them to one side of my saddle, the outing flannel in a flour sack to the other. With my white dress rolled up around my waist over my khaki riding skirt, I rode to Martha's for the wedding dinner. She came running into the yard to meet me, holding her veil and her embroidered new dress up out of the dry manure dust with her farm-girl hands in elbow-length white silk gloves. I was overwhelmed by her strangeness, and couldn't do anything except push the peonies at her. Of course she couldn't take them, not with her gloves, and so I carried the flowers to the house and arranged them in a blue crock with Martha giving the advice. This helped us both through the embarrassment of the outing-flannel present and into the dinner, which was delayed by a discussion about the gloves. Should the bride eat with them on or might she take them off? By this time the groom got to making enough noise so that I had to notice him.

"Off!" was his firm verdict about the gloves. No use having to wash them right away. They would last a long time, years, if Martha took care of them as his sisters did theirs—laid them away in blue paper to keep out the light. As the talk went around the table I looked the man over. He was that bleak age which the twenties are to the middle teens. His hair was clipped far above his ears in a highwater cut, as we called it, his knobby head showing blue around the back. The collar propping up his cleft chin was real linen, but the suit looked wooly as Grandfather's old wedding broadcloth in our trunk at home. Yet Martha seemed to like her man very much, with all his talk of "the little flat I got feathered for my little bird—" which I considered sickeningly mushy. Nor did I think he came up to any of my dancing partners, not even the one who always puffed so in the schottisches because a horse fell on him when he was small and smashed something inside.

After everybody was full of dinner and there was nothing more to do, things got particularly bad for me, with all the old-country wedding jokes and horseplay. So I managed to slip out to the clearer air of the porch. After a while Martha found me and with an arm around my back as in the old days, she looked into the yard where her flea-bitten pony stomped at the flies. And as in the old days she whispered a secret into my ear. It was about her mother. With only one daughter to be married off, she wouldn't let Martha have the dinner she wanted, with both bride's cake and *kolaches*.

"My one big day—" Martha said, blinking at the bank of tears in her blue eyes.

I tried to tell her that it didn't matter, not out here in the hills, but all I could think about was this unknown woman beside me, talking about such foolish things as bride's cake and *kolaches*, making an important secret of them. She saw my silence for something else and suddenly the kindness that was the Martha I knew broke through all the grown-up woman air of the dress and the day. Laughing out loud as when she was eleven, she said that we must make a charm to bring us together again some day. She would leave me a piece of her hair that I used to love so much. Before I had to say anything she gathered up her veil over her arm and was gone to get the scissors.

But I didn't have to take the hair, for Martha's new husband followed her out and standing between us, an arm around each, reminded us that he must now be asked about everything. Maybe I'd better give him a kiss too, just to make sure he would say yes. I pulled away but no one was watching me, particularly not the old people inside the house, who were laughing, taking sides, the women encouraging Martha.

"Go ahead, cut it off. Right at the start you have to show him—" they called to her. But the men shouted them down, slapping their knees in approval at the new husband's firm stand. By golly, you could see who would rule that roost—

So the newlyweds argued a little, pouted and kissed, and then went into the house to sit on the bench along the wall while a pitcher of wine was passed around and the father played the accordion. As soon as I could I said something about going home.

"You know how the folks are about me being off the doorstep a second—"

Martha knew. It was a wonder they had let me come at all, the very first time I ever managed to get away without some special errand to be done for my father. So I shook hands awkwardly all around and went to put on my riding skirt. I hated walking through the room with it hanging out below my white dress, but there was no back door. When I finally got to my horse Martha came running through the yard, her veil flying loose behind.

"Oh, I hate to go—to leave everything!" she cried, her gentle eyes swimming.

At last I got away, and as my shaggy little buckskin

carried me across the wide meadow, I thought of that fine springtime on the old Niobrara when we used to lie awake nights in the attic, telling stories, Martha's always of beautiful maidens, and princes who were bewitched into frogs or cold wet stones; whispering the stories carefully so the baby wouldn't waken or Mother hear us from downstairs. But that was when I was little, a long time ago, and today the sun was shining and the first prairie roses were pink and fragrant on the upland side of the road. On the marshy side mallard ducks and their young chattered in the rushes, or dove in the open water, busy with their feeding.

And at the fence beyond the first rise a top buggy was waiting, one of the red-wheeled ones from Martha's old crowd.

"Maybe you think I got to have an automobile—?" the serious young German settler complained when I wouldn't ride in the buggy with him, although I did let my horse idle alongside while I teased the man a little for being such a slow-poke, letting an outsider come in and take Martha away.

At the next dance I ate supper with one of my hay waddies as usual—an art student from Chicago who brought me *Lord Jim* to read and had no cookstove for a bride, no place of his own at all, not even a saddlehorse. But he was teaching me a new kind of fox trot, and anyway I knew that I could have those other things if I wanted them, for now I was really grown-up, with a bachelor in a red-wheeled buggy waiting for me along the road.

Of course I still didn't have thick yellow braids to hang as far as my knees, but that hadn't mattered for a long time.

Marlizzie

The American Frontier is gone, we like to say, a little sadly. And with it went the frontier woman who followed her man along the dusty trail of the buffalo into the land of the hostile Indian. Never again will there be a woman like the wife of Marcus Whitman, who, exactly a hundred years ago, looked out upon a thousand miles of empty West from the bows of a wagon rolling up the Platte toward Oregon.

But there was a later, a less spectacular, and a much more persistent frontier in America, a frontier of prairie fire, drouth, and blizzard, a frontier of land fights and sickness and death far from a doctor, yet with all the characteristic gaiety, deep friendships, and that personal freedom so completely incomprehensible to the uninitiated.

Among my acquaintances are many women who walked the virgin soil of such a frontier and made good lives for themselves and those about them. And when they could they did not turn their backs upon the land they struggled to conquer. They stayed, refusing to be told that they occupy the last fringes of a retreating civilization, knowing that life there can be good and bountiful.

One of these frontierswomen is Marlizzie, living more than thirty miles from a railroad, over towering sandhills and through valleys that deepen and broaden to hayflats, with scarcely a house and not a tree the whole way.

No matter when you may come, you will find her away somewhere: chasing a turkey hen, looking after the cattle, repairing fence with stretchers and staples, trimming trees in the orchard, or perhaps piling cow chips for winter fuel. A blow or two on the old steel trap spring that hangs in place of a dinner bell at the gate will bring her—running, it seems to strangers, but really only at her usual gait, a gait that none of the six children towering over her can equal.

She comes smiling and curious, shading her faded blue eyes to see who you may be, and eager to welcome you in any event. And as she approaches, you see her wonderful wiry slightliness, notice that her forearms, always bare, are like steel with twisted cables under dark leather—with hands that are beautiful in the knotted vigor that has gripped the hoe and the pitchfork until the fingers can never be straightened, fingers that still mix the ingredients for the world's most divine concoction—Swiss plum pie.

And while you talk in the long kitchen–living room, she listens eagerly, demanding news of far places—the Rhineland, not so far from the place of her birth; Africa, and the political games in the Far East. Apologetically she explains that the mail is slow and uncertain here. Her daily papers come a sackful at a time, and there is no telephone. Besides, the decayed old stock station thirty miles away is little more than a post office and shipping pens. News still travels in the frontier manner, by word of mouth.

And while Marlizzie listens, perhaps she will make you a pie or two or even three—for one piece, she is certain, would be an aggravation. Gently she tests the plums between her fingers, choosing only the firmest, to halve and pit and lay in ring after ring like little saucers into crust-lined tins. Then sugar and enough of the custard, her own recipe, to cover the plums to dark submerged circles. She dots the top with thick sweet cream, dusts it with nutmeg, or if you insist—but it is a serious sacrilege—with cinnamon, and slips them into her Nile-green range, gleaming as a rare piece of porcelain and heated to the exact degree with corncobs. And as she works, her hair, that she had so carefully smoothed with water before she began the pies, has come up in a halo of curls, still with a bright, glinting brown in it for all her sixty-nine years.

It is a little difficult to see in this Marlizzie, so like a timberline tree but stanchly erect, the woman of forty years ago, delicate of skin with white hands, and what was known as "style" in the days of the leg-o'-mutton sleeve, the basque, and the shirred taffeta front. She came hopefully to Western Nebraska with eight new dresses of cashmeres and twills and figured French serges in navy, brown, gray, and green. One had a yard and a half in each sleeve, and one—a very fine light navy—had two yards of changeable gold-and-blue taffeta pleated into the front of the basque. Marlizzie got so many because she suspected that it might be difficult to find good tailoring, with good style and cloth, right at the first in this wilderness. It was, and still is; but she found no occasion for the clothes she brought, or the renewal of her wardrobe with anything except calico or denim. Gradually the fine dresses were cut up for her children.

Within three months of the day that she struggled with her absurd rosetted little hat in the wind that swept the border town and all the long road to her home in the jolting lumber wagon, Marlizzie had ceased for all time to be a city woman. She had learned to decoy the wily team of Indian ponies and had converted, without a sewing machine, a fashionable gray walking skirt and cape into a pair of trousers and a cap for her new husband.

Ten years later her children found the tape loops once used to hold the trailing widths of the skirt from the dust of the street. When they asked what the loops were for, she told them and laughed a little as she buttoned her denim jacket to go out and feed the cattle. She had married an idealist, a visionary who dreamed mightily of a Utopia and worked incessantly to establish his dream and forgot that cattle must be fed to stand the white cold of thirty-below-zero weather.

By the time the calluses of her hands were as horn, her arms gnarling, and she had somehow fed every hungry wayfarer that came to her door, she had learned many things—among them that on the frontier democracy was an actuality and that, despite the hardships, there was a wonderful plentitude of laughter and singing, often with dancing until the cows bawled for their morning milking, or winter-long storytelling around the heater red with cow chips.

The six children of Marlizzie were brought into the world and into maturity whole and sound without a doctor in the house. Though sugar was a luxury and bread often made from grain she ground in a hand mill, they were fed. Despite the constant menace of rattlesnakes to bare feet, and range cattle and wild horses and the dare-deviltry the frontier engenders in its young, not one of the children lost so much as a little finger.

Marlizzie learned the arts of the frontier: butchering, meat care, soapmaking, and the science of the badger-oil lamp, with its underwear wick speared on a hairpin. Stores were remote, even had there been money. Not for twenty-five years, not until she was subpoenaed on a murder case, was she on a train. Finally in 1926 she was in town long enough to see her first moving picture. She stayed in the dark little opera house all the afternoon and the evening to see it over and over, and talked of it as she talked so long ago about the wonders of *Faust*.

During those years Marlizzie saw many spring suns rise upon the hills as she ran through the wet grass for the team, or stopped to gather a handful of wild sweet peas for her daughter, who was tied to the babies and had little time for play. Often before the fall dawnings Marlizzie stripped the milk from her cow. It was far to the field, and she and her husband must put in long days to husk the little corn before the snow came.

In those forty years Marlizzie saw large herds of range cattle driven into the country, their horns like a tangled thicket over a flowing dusty blanket of brown. She saw them give way to the white-faced Hereford, and the thick-skinned black cattle that crawled through all her fences. She saw the hard times of the East push the settler westward and the cattleman arm against the invasion. She helped mold bullets for the settlers' defense or listened silently, her knitting needles flying, to the latest account of a settler shot down between the plow handles or off his windmill before the eyes of his wife and children.

She knitted only a little more rapidly when it was her own man that was threatened, her brother-in-law that was shot. And always there was patching to be done when her husband was away for weeks on settler business and she could not sleep. In the earlier days, when there was no money for shoes, she made the slippers for the little ones from old overalls on these nights, making a double agony of it. Nothing hurt her pride more than the badly shod feet of her children.

She dug fence-post holes along lines of virgin land, hoed corn, fought prairie fires. She saw three waves of population, thousands of families, come into the free-land region, saw two-thirds of them turn back the next day and more dribble back as fast as they could get money from the folks back home, until only a handful remained.

Marlizzie still lives on the old homestead. With a hired hand—a simple, smiling boy—she runs the place that she helped build through the long years with those gnarled hands. Now that her husband has planned his last ideal community, even the larger decisions are hers to make: the time for the haying, the branding and vaccinating of the cattle, the replacing of trees in her orchards. As the frontier women before her, she looks to the sky and the earth, and their signs do not fail her.

The last time I saw Marlizzie at her home she was on a high ladder, painting the new barn built from the lumber of the old one that the wind destroyed. Winter was coming, but in her vegetable pit was enough produce for herself and her neighbors until spring, with jellies and vegetables and fruit and even roast turkey in glass jars. And in the barn, swathed in a clean old sheet, hung a yearling beef that she and the hired hand had killed and dressed.

Tomorrow she was going to town, a 120-mile trip in a son's truck, to the nearest town large enough to carry husking mittens and the things she needed for Christmas. Then there must be the special bits for the Thanksgiving dinner, such as dates, nuts, and cranberries and a few candies and other goodies.

Most of the dinner will be of her own growing. Always she roasts the largest young tom turkey from her noisy flock. The turkey is eked out with perhaps a couple of pheasants or capons and some catfish dipped from the barrel of running water where she has been fattening them all fall. And toward noon on Thanksgiving day the uninvited guests will begin to come, and come most of the afternoon, until every dish has been washed several times and the last comer fed in true frontier fashion.

And then they will all gather around the old organ, played by one of the daughters of Marlizzie. They will go through the old song books until they are all weary and sentimental and very sad and happy. Toward evening someone will surely come running. Perhaps a gate has been left open; the cattle have broken into the stackyards or a horse is sick. And Marlizzie will tuck up her skirts and fly to the emergency, much as she did the time a three-hundred-pound neighbor came down with a burst appendix and there was nothing better than the sheet-covered kitchen table for the emergency operation, with Marlizzie to stand by the doctor.

Or she will fly to the help of the new frontier woman. Economic stringency has always given the more sparsely settled regions the miraginal aspects of a refuge. During the past five years remote habitations have sprung up on deserted or isolated tracts of land that lay unclaimed.

This newer woman of the frontier lives in a log house, a soddy, a dugout, or even a haystack, much as her predecessors. Thrust from a factory, office, or from the bridge table, she comes alone or with a husband also the victim of the times. Often strong from tennis or swimming she can lay sod, hew a log, or dig a dugout, day in and out, beside most men. She learns to cook over an open fire or in a dutch oven, and, if necessary, to make an oil lamp with a wick from her husband's sock, cut round and round, and speared on an unbent hairpin across a sardine can.

I saw one of these new homemakers in the south sandhills of Nebraska not so long ago. Twenty miles from the nearest boxcar depot, an old Model T without a top, fender, or windshield drew out of the rutted trail to let us pass. In place of an engine the motive power was an old flea-bitten mare, the single-tree slack against her hoary fetlocks. The car body was rounded into a neatly tiered mound of cow chips, the native coal of the sandhills. In front, his feet reaching down to brace against the dash, sat the driver, a young man in frayed-bottom trousers. In the back was a young woman in overalls and an orange felt hat that still carried a hint of the jauntiness of a good shop. Beside her was the battered old washtub used to gather the fuel.

As we passed, they acknowledged our greeting with the salute of the hills, hand in air, palm out. A mile farther on, in a half-acre pocket, was the home of the new settlers: a low structure of Russian thistles and bunch grass tamped between layers of old chicken wire for the walls, held up by posts. There was one glassless window and a door, and through the thatch of brush on the roof rose an old stove-pipe chimney with screen tied over it. Against the north side of the little house hung the pelts of a litter of half-grown coyotes, and drying from the clothesline were wreaths of green beans, covered with the skirt of a wash-faded voile dress. In a low plot spaded from the tough sod grew beans and late turnips and rutabagas and Chinese winter radishes. In a square pen shaded with an armful of weeds across a corner, a fine red shoat slept.

I felt a glow of recognition as we passed. These people were already my people. From Marlizzie and her kind they were learning all the tricks of wresting a living, even a good life, from this last frontier.

For amusement the young woman in the orange hat will go to the sandhill dances with others of her kind, perhaps in an outmoded party dress, but most likely in a mail-order print, perhaps made by hand or on the sewing machine of Marlizzie. Their men will be in overalls, turned up jauntily at the cuffs, with open shirt necks and loose ties.

The women will sit on planks over boxes along the wall as their grandmothers did. Now and then the older women, like Marlizzie, will dance to the same fiddle and accordion of forty, fifty years ago. And at midnight there will be cake and sandwiches and coffee.

And toward morning the crowd will scatter, on horse-back, in wagons, and in a few old cars that cough and sputter in the sand. The women go to their homes, the straw ticks and cottonwood-leaf mattresses, and to refreshing sleep.

They are not so different from Marlizzie or even the wife of Marcus Whitman. They, too, will learn to look to the sky for the time of planting and harvest, to the earth for the wisdom and the strength she yields to those who walk her freshly turned sod.

Sandhill Sundays

Out of the East and the South, God's country, came the movers, pounding their crowbait ponies or their logy plow critters on to the open range of Northwest Nebraska. They exchanged green grass, trees, and summer night rains for dun-colored sandhills crowding upon each other far into the horizon, wind singing in the red bunch grass or howling over the snow-whipped knobs of December, and the heat devils of July dancing over the hard land west of the hills. No Indian wars, few gun fights with bad men or wild animals—mostly it was just standing off the cold and scratching for grub. And lonesome! Dog owls, a few nesters in dugouts or soddies, dusty cow waddies loping over the hills, and time dragging at the heels—every day Monday.

Then came big doings. Cow towns with tent and false-front saloons; draw played Sunday afternoons in the dust of the trail between the shacks; cowboys tearing past the little sod churches, shooting the air full of holes while the sky pilots inside prayed hell and damnation on them; settlers cleaned of their shirts by cardsharpers whilst their women picked cow chips barefooted and corn leaves rattled dry in the wind.

When the settlers got clear down in the mouth, the sky pilots showed up among them. The meeting-point of the revivals was most generally Alkali Lake, on the Flats. All Sunday morning moving wagons, horsebackers, hoofers, and a buggy or two from town collected along the bare bank. Almost every dugout or claim shack for twenty, thirty miles around was deserted. Everybody turned out to hear the walking parson.

From the back end of a buggy, fortified by a beard cut like that of Christ in holy pictures, the sky pilot lined out the crowd hunched over on wagon tongues, stretched on horse blankets or on the ground, hot with the glaring sun.

"You see them heat waves out there on the prairie? Them's the fires of hell, licking round your feet, burning your feet, burning your faces red as raw meat, drying up your crops, drawing the water out of your wells! You see them thunderheads, shining like mansions in the sky but spurting fire and shaking the ground under your feet? God is mad, mad as hell!"

Somewhere a woman began to moan and cry. The crowd was up like a herd of longhorns at the smell of fire. A swarthy groundscratcher from down on the Breaks began to sing "Nearer My God to Thee," couldn't remember the words, and broke out crying, too. Others took up songs. "Beulah Land." Somebody broke into the popular parody and hid his face. "Washed in the Blood of the Lamb."

Two whiskered grangers helped the parson off the buggy. "Come to Jesus! Come to Jesus!" he sang as he waded into the already cooling water of the lake. The moaning woman was ducked first and came up sputtering and coughing. The crowd pushed forward, to the bank, into the water.

And when the sun slipped away and the cool wind carried the smell to stale water weed over the prairie, almost everybody was saved. Mrs. Schmidt, with eight children and a husband usually laid out in the saloon at Hay Springs, sang all the way home she was so happy. The next week they sent her to the insane asylum. The youngest Frahm girl took pneumonia from the ten-mile trip behind plow critters and died. The lone Bohemian who scratched the thin ground on the Breaks strung himself up.

Talk of the big revival drifted back into the hills. "I wisht I coulda gone; it'd-a been a lot of comfort to me," Mrs. Endow mumbled when she heard about it. But one of their horses had died of botts and her only chance of getting out now was in a pine box.

II

The nesters, well versed in drainage, were helpless against the drouth. Each spring there was less money for seed, and Sundays were more and more taken up with the one problem, irrigation. Everybody threw in together here, the Iowa farmer, the New England schoolteacher afraid of his horses, and the worn-out desert rat, the European intellectual, and the Southern poor white. There was no place for women at these meetings and so they stayed at home, wrangling the old hen and chickens and watering the dry sticks of hollyhock.

Ten years later the drouth, the cold, and too much buying on pump had driven out the shallow-rooted nesters and the sky pilots. A few hilltop churches took care of those who still believed in a benevolent God. The stickers took up dry farming, pailed cows, and ran cattle. But farming and milking meant long hours; ranching called for large pastures and consequent isolation. Night entertainment grew more common. First came literaries, with windy debates on Popular Election of Our Presidents and the British Colonial Policy, followed by spelldowns and a program—songs: "Love is Such a Funny, Funny Thing," "Oh, Bury Me Not on the Lone Prairie"; dialogues;

pieces: "The Deacon's Courtship" and "The Face on the Barroom Floor"; food. Then the long trails across the hills, dangerous at night, particularly along the gullies and river bluffs.

Eventually most of the communities settled upon dancing as the most conducive to all-night entertainment. Everybody went. If Old John was running the floor at the dance, there'd be a shapping match if he had to cuss out every cowhand or bean-eater there. He'd begin to look the crowd over while he was calling the square dances:

> Gents bow out and ladies bow under,
> Hug 'em up tight and swing like thunder

—up on an old tub or bench, stomping his boots to hurry the fiddlers until the girls' feet left the floor and skirts flew. At midnight he'd help carry in the wash boiler full of coffee, dip a tin cup among the floating sacks of grounds, and pour it back through the steam.

"Looks like your coffee fell in a crick coming over," he always bawled out. Nobody except Mrs. Beal, Old Man Beal's mail-order wife, ever minded.

With his cud of Battle Ax stowed away in a little rawhide sack he carried, Old John would sink his freed jaws into a thick slab of boiled ham and bread as he helped pass the dishpans full of sandwiches and cake to couples lining the walls, sitting on boards laid between chairs. The remains in the pans he'd distribute among the stags sitting on horse blankets, like flies gathered about drops of sorghum on the floor. And afterward, while he swept the dust and bread rinds into little piles, he'd egg on the shapping match.

"Times ain't like they was," he'd complain, looking the crowd over. "There ain't a feller here with spunk 'nuff to take a leatherin' to git a purty girl."

Somebody who didn't bring a girl but would like to

take one home finally grinned and stood up, his neck getting red when the prettier girls, those that might be chosen,
giggled. And somebody who was afraid of losing his girl,
or had a general prod on, got up too, and the bargain was
made.

A horsebacker's leather shaps are brought in and un-
laced so the two legs fall apart. Each shapper takes half and
the crowd follows them to the middle of the floor, Old
John passing out advice impartially between trips to the
door to spit.

Coats, if any, are jerked off, collars unbuttoned. Norm
and Al, the two shappers, sit on the floor, facing, their legs
dove-tailed, each with half a shap. Everybody crowds up,
the dancers first, then the older folks, and around the edge
the boys and dogs.

They draw straws from Old John's fist and the unlucky
one, Norm, lies on his back and snaps his legs up over him.
He takes the horsehide across his rump with all the sting
Al can spread on it. Al's legs are up now; Norm gets his
lick in on saddle-hardened muscles. The crowd yells. The
whack-whack of the shaps settles down into a steady clock-
work business, the legs going up and down like windmill
rods. After a while Al jerks his head and Old John drags
him out. He sits up, his face red and streaked as a homesick
school-ma'am's, only his is sweating.

"Norm's got two pairs of pants on."

The accused is taken out and fetched back. "Only one
pair," says Old John. The whacking starts again. Girls
giggle nervously, their men hanging to them. The crowd
is taking sides. Two sprouts near the edge take a lam at
each other. Old John separates them. On the floor the
whacking is slowing up. He drags Al away again, the
puncher's head lolling, his face gray as window putty.

The crowd shies back. A pail of water is brought in. Al's
face is wet down with a towel. He grunts and turns over

on his belly, the sign that Norm's won. Who'll he pick? There's no hurry. He can't dance any more tonight and it's a long time until "Home, Sweet Home."

Everybody is talking. The fiddlers start:

> Honor your partner and don't be afraid
> To swing corner lady in a waltz promenade.

Sunday was spent getting home and sleeping.

III

As the nesters pulled out, sheepmen bought in along the fringe of the hills. Here and there a settler who couldn't make a go of the newer farming or cattle took up woolie culture too, and then the coyote, up to now a raider of hen coops and scrub calves, developed into a killer. Wolf hunts were organized. The regular hour for a hunt was about nine in the morning. A relay of shots started the horse-backers off on a fifteen-mile front, from Mirage Flats to Keplinger's Bridge. Yelling, whistling, running any coyote that tried to break the line, they headed for Jackson's towards a big V made of hog wire, chicken fencing, and lath corncribbing with a wire trap in the point.

Broad-handed women unpacked baskets of grub in the big barn now for the dinner.

"Time they was rounding up a few coyotes," Mrs. Putney says, as she uncovers a roaster full of browned chickens. "Henry lost twenty-five sheep last week, just killed and let lay."

"They been having three, four hunts a year since '84 and all they does is make the critters harder to catch. They nearly never gets none," Mary Bowen, an old settler, commented as she measured out the ground coffee. "Dogs or poison, that fixes the sneaking devils that gets my turkeys."

"But where's the fun in that?" asked one of the girls

climbing into the mow, late, but not dressed for work, anyway.

By one o'clock black specks are running over the Flats like bugs. Yells, commands, a cloud of dust. Horses tromping on each other's heels. A few shots. That's all.

Four rabbits, one badger, and two coyotes for two hundred hunters.

"Got sight of a couple of more, but they musta snuck outa the lines. Not many-a the Pine Creek bunch showed up."

Now the dinner, dished up on long boards over barrels in the mow. Windy fellows talking about long-ago hunts, when there were real wolves, too smart for a mob. Cigars were passed by the local candidate for the legislature; an invitation to a hunt at Rushville two weeks come Sunday was read, and the hunt was over.

IV

But the grass in the loose soil died under the sharp hoofs and close cropping of the woolies. The ranchers hated sheep and made it as hot for the woolie nurses as they could. At last most of the sheepmen pulled their freight. But just as the country was going back to cows, the Kinkaid Act was passed. The land rush put a shack on every section of land—Easterners mostly, who established Sunday schools, with ladies' aids to meet Sunday afternoons because the horses must work on weekdays. Many of the newcomers objected to dancing and had play-parties instead. The soddies were small and the Kinkaider chose his games accordingly. Charades, guessing games, or

> Tin-tin,
> Come in,
> Want to buy some tin?

Perhaps

> Pleased or displeased?
> Displeased.
> What can I do to please you?

Foot races, pussy wants a corner, drop the handkerchief, or all outs in free on moonlit summer evenings. And endless songs, many of them parodies on popular tunes:

> Al Reneau was a ranchman's name,
> Skinning Kinkaiders was his game,
> First mortgages only, at a high percent,
> Jew you down on your cattle to the last red cent.

But no matter how much truck the Kinkaider grew, he couldn't turn it into cash profitably unless it could walk the thirty, forty miles to a shipping point. They must have a railroad. Once more the women stayed at home while the men gathered at the local post office, chewed tobacco, talked, wrote letters, signed petitions, and bought more machinery on pump, on the hope of a railroad that never came. Once more the shallow-rooted left and the rest turned into combination farmers and stockmen. Sundays became ranch days, with a new crop of cowpunchers to show off before the native daughters at scratching matches.

The crowd is perched on the top planks, on the up-wind side of the corral. Here Monkey Ward cowboys strut about in bat wings and loud shirts. Riders that are riders sit on their haunches in the sun, dressed in worn shaps and blue shirts. In the corral several green hands are running a handful of wild-eyed colts around, trying for a black gelding. They snag an old sorrel mare, have to throw her to get the rope, try again.

"Why don't y'u do y'ur practisin' on y'ur bucket calves to home?" an old-timer laughs, nudging his straw-chewing neighbor. Dust, mix-up of horses and booted cowboys.

They have the gelding, snub him short. Now for the blind and the leather. Red climbs on the last horse, the drawing card of the Sunday afternoon.

"Let 'er go!"

The corral gate flies back. The blind's jerked away. The black shakes, gathers into a hump, pushing Red up into the sky.

"Rip him open!"

The spurs rowel a red arc on the black hide. The horse goes up, turns, hits the dust headed north, and it's over. Red's still going south.

A hazer snags the horse, not head-shy, and brings him in. The fence hoots when Red gets up, dusts off his new hat, and walks away to himself. Not even hurt.

Lefty is prodded off the fence, not so keen now as he was a minute before Red lit. He climbs on. The black, instead of going up, spraddles out, sinking his smoke belly to the ground.

"Scratch him!" an old-timer shouts. Lefty does. The horse is off across the prairie, bucking and running in a straight line. That's nothing. But he stops short, all four feet together. Lefty comes near going on.

"Fan him!" a tenderfoot shouts. An old rider spits. His guess is correct. There isn't time for fanning. The black leaves the ground, swaps ends, runs, swaps again. Lefty hangs on as best he can but the turns come too fast. He's down on his shoulder, just missing the double kick the black lets out before he quits the country. Lefty picks himself up, his arm hanging funny.

"Collarbone's busted."

A couple of girls in overalls slide off the fence and fuss over Lefty. Any rider's a good rider while he's hurt.

"That horse belongs in a rodeo string," they comfort him.

The fence is deserted. "See you all at my place tonight!"

Madge Miller shouts. The young people scatter down the valley in little knots and couples. Some shag it over the chophills, hurrying home to do the chores so they can go to the party at Madge's.

"Next scratching match at the Bar M week come Sunday," someone reminds the riders.

"Hi!"

V

The country is scarcely grown up and people are already building a tradition, a background. Old settlers and their children are suddenly superior to newer settlers and entitled to an annual barbecue as befits the honor. An old-time roundup dust hangs over Peck's Grove. Horses shy and snort at the smell of fire and frying meat. Cars are lined up by the signal stick of Mike Curran, who once prodded cows through the branding chute. Cowboys tear up, leading wild horses for the bucking contest.

"Hi! Gonna ride that snaky bronc? Betcha two bits you can't even sit my old broomtail!"

Women hurry about, lugging heavy baskets, picking a shady place for the old settlers' table. The men look over the race track, the horses, the new cars.

"Well, you son of a sand turtle! Step down and look at your saddle!"

Logan-Pomroy grins and gets out of his imported car. He shakes the hand of Old Amos, champion muskrat trapper, for this one day a year forgetting that he is the owner of a ranch and three banks and that Amos is in dirty overalls, with gunny sack and baling wire for shoes. Today they are old cronies, the two oldest settlers.

"How's the meat hole coming?" Logan-Pomroy demands, and leads the way to the barbecue pit. Two sweating ranch cooks are turning quarters of browning beef with pitchforks or basting the meat carefully with a mixture of water, vinegar, salt, and pepper. The drippings sizzle and smoke in the red bed of ash-wood coals in the pit under the barbecuing racks.

"Come and git it!" a fat woman calls after what seems hours.

The men trail over to a table made of salt barrels and planks covered with white cloths. At the head Logan-Pomroy and Amos sit, with later settlers down the sides. Old settlers' daughters wait on them, passing huge platters of beef, mutton, and pork, followed by unlimited vegetables, salads, pies, cake, fruit, and several rounds of the coffeepot.

After dinner there'll be contests. Fat men's, sack, three-legged, potato, and peanut races. For the women there is that old rip-snorter, a wagon race. Each contestant draws two horses, a wagon, and enough harness. First to drive around the track wins. The young cowboys with hair on their chests will show their guts in the bucking-bronco contest, twisting the broncs in approved style, and take part in the wild cow, wild mule, and surcingle races. But before that there are cigars and speeches and songs. Old Amos adds his rumblings to the "Nebraska Land":

> I've reached the land of drouth and heat,
> Where nothing grows for man to eat.
> For wind that blows with burning heat,
> Nebraska Land is hard to beat.

About sundown the crowd scatters. Logan-Pomroy's motor roars up the hill. Without a good-bye Old Amos shuffles away through the brush down the river. The big day is over.

VI

But the sandhiller lives in the present also. The young folks take long car trips to dances that break up at midnight, by command of the law, and endeavor to spend most of the time until Sunday morning getting home. Sunday is a good day for those who need it to sleep off bad liquor. The more prosperous ranchers escape the cold by going south, the heat by going to the lakes. Some of these are old settlers noted for forty years of unfailing hospitality. They still entertain, when they are home, in comfortable ranch houses with refrigerators and radios. Once their invitations, usually printed in the local items of the community paper, read something like this:

NOTICE

Party and dance at Bud Jennet's, April 2.

Dinner from one to seven.

Beds and breakfast for all.

Everybody welcome.

Seventy, eighty people would come in those days, some of them forty miles in wagons or on horseback. Next day the men slept between suggans in the haymow, the women all over the house. But that was when Yvette was a baby. Now she is home from college and with formal bids, as she calls them, they rounded up twenty guests for about four hours of housewarming in their new home. Some of them came a hundred miles, and it was worth the trip. There is an orchestra in the music room, with flowers from Alliance, and candles, Japanese prints framed in Chinese red, and tapestry panels.

"Such a beautiful home!" the guests exclaim to Mrs. Jennet.

And in three hours the maid has the muss all cleared away.

There is no disputing the fact that the Jennets did well in cattle and potash. The callers were all prosperous and charming. Not like the Jennets' guests once were, when all who read the notice were welcome. Today nobody ate with starvation appetite. Nobody had to be thawed out at the hay-burner before he could sing "The Little Old Sod Shanty on the Claim" or play "There'll Be a Hot Time" on the fiddle or the accordion. Nobody let habitual curses slip and surely none of the guests today would ever think of stomping and singing:

> Just plant me in a stretch of west,
> Where coyotes mourn their kin.
> Let hawses paw and tromp the mound
> But don't you fence it in.

These people believe in sealed copper coffins in vaults, and they are decidedly not planted but laid to rest. And not one of them forgot himself so far as to ask about Bud Jennet, knowing that he must be in Alliance with his new lady friend, seeing that he wasn't to the housewarming.

Outpost in New York

The first thing I hung on my wall in Greenwich Village was my cowboy hat. It had been a cheap one in the first place and now it was old and burn-stained from the time it helped save me and my horse from a prairie fire, years ago, but hanging it seemed a sort of commitment to stay in New York for a few months, and a reminder, in moments of anger and disgust with the east, that there was another country and another people.

On previous trips to New York I had always stayed at some hotel, perhaps, if I followed the publisher's suggestions, at the Chatham, a sort of second home for Kathleen Norris, Mignon Eberhart, and other highly successful writers. More often I checked into the old Lincoln, near Times Square, close to the theaters and the Public Library, and with good subway connections in the basement. I knew that publishers disapproved of the Lincoln and that a few violent characters did hang out there, including some involved with the old Dutch Schultz gang, but the telephone service was remarkable. Besides, after a childhood in the later cattleman-settler troubles of the west, one gunman more or less among the thousands of people drifting through the lobby of the Lincoln didn't seem very alarming.

I got a glimpse of the general attitude toward the hotel

when I picked up a cab at Grand Central Station one dawn, with the Boston train checks still on my luggage.

"The Lincoln Hotel, please," I said, ready for a little sleep.

"Lincoln?" the driver inquired, turning clear around, giving my bags and me a New York cabman's look. "O.K., just so long's you don't get above the fourteenth floor."

I may be mistaken about the number of the floor after all these years but I recall the rest of the comment and the tone of voice very clearly. I never went above the fourteenth floor or wherever the drift line was, not then or during a dozen later visits, and I still feel a little awkward about this lack of daring. After all, a younger brother and I, lost with our frightened little old-country grandmother in a violent thunderstorm, had spent a night at a roadranch where, it was rumored, a man who went in might never come out again, and that it was even possible to get a bullet in the back from the roadranch guns while far from the premises (as happened to our uncle a short time later).

Although Grandmother spoke no English and my brother and I were only five and six at the time, we knew the rumors, at least the worst ones, and realized that the Winchester our father always carried was against such people. Still, the women of the ranch gave us soft beds and a fine breakfast, with a jackknife at my brother's plate and a red ribbon at mine. We saw nothing of fresh diggings where bodies might be buried, but we believed that the signs must have been washed away in the hard rain during the night.

I made the Lincoln Hotel my headquarters for several weeks each year until the winter of 1942–43, when I came east to put in some time on home front propaganda work. That meant living in Washington or New York and the latter seemed less crowded. Still, the agencies either had no apartments or considered me a bad risk and certainly a tightfisted one, for I offered no "gold behind the palm," as the old timers out west used to call it. With the determination of a home-seeking immigrant I kept looking. There was a two-and-a-half-room apartment up on West Seventy-fifth Street, with a nice little garden in the back, but my appearance seemed to cause a flutter among the women showing the place. There were signs and glances, and whisperings in German.

"How is it that she comes here?" and "Who has then sent her?"

This was puzzling, for certainly they couldn't know anything about me except that I wasn't a New Yorker, although Douglas Gilbert had once described me as looking like something out of Edith Wharton, which wouldn't be New York, not the city.

The women became less and less enthusiastic about me. They did let me glance into the bathroom while holding the door open about six inches. I insisted on trying the hot water and noticed, behind the high-footed old tub, a large colored picture of Hitler, perhaps thrust there hastily, out of sight of anyone except a tall-eyed snooper from the west.

Then there was the "elegant one-room studio" familiar to every apartment seeker in New York. This one was off lower Fifth Avenue, the raised platform across one end of the room filled by a huge Hollywood bed, covered in gold rayon satin with a pile of blue cushions. The shower and stool were jammed into a narrow closet and an electric plate behind a box was the kitchen. It was shabbier than my eight dollar a month room back in Lincoln, Nebraska, in my college days, but then I didn't have a Hollywood bed.

Just when the apartment search seemed hopeless, someone told me about a little agency on West Fourth, in

Greenwich Village. It was owned by two rather fabulous women, complete loves. They were elderly road-show actresses from somewhere around Minnesota or Wisconsin and had appeared, it seemed, in every little opera house and show tent across all of America and remembered the most remote little tank towns in exact and affectionate detail. Because this was January, 1943, they had little to offer except gay conversation. After a while, preceded by some scribbled notes passed between the two, and a few heavy glances, they wondered aloud whether an Italian with a small apartment house a couple of blocks away might be willing to "clean up his fourth floor."

By this time I wasn't too sure what such cleaning might entail, whether varmints, insects or people, or just plain dirt, but I agreed to go look. The ladies called the landlord and after some rather curious persuasion by both of them on one telephone, we were told to come over. We waited at the door of the man's apartment on the first floor for a long time. Finally a mild-mannered and polite little Italian came out and led us, with considerable reluctance, up the darkish stairs to the fourth floor.

"I don't know—" he was still saying as he turned the key.

The place was full of dust, several years of New York soot and dust, but there were three long front windows, and a fireplace that worked. The nice sweep of wall space was cut into panels of faded pink with huge red roses wreathing each panel—hand-painted roses, with a flower on each of the many small panes in the casement windows that opened to the inside bedroom.

"Looks like a deserted love nest," I said, thinking about the stories one hears about New York in New York.

There was no apparent notice of my remark. The ladies were busy pointing out the big storage space above the closet, and the full-sized window in the bathroom, with roses around it too. All this time the landlord stood in the middle of the floor, silent, his shoe soles deep in dust, their tops white with plaster from some other apartment.

Finally the two ladies marched upon the mild man and although he backed away until the wall stopped him, he finally agreed to lease the place.

"Yeh, yeh," he said wearily, "I'll paint—"

"Can you furnish it?" I asked. "I don't want to buy furniture here."

He shook his head, brightening a little, but one of the ladies was still fast with a cue. Oh, furniture was no problem, she said. There was a man over in Brooklyn, retired army colonel, who ran a sort of antique second-hand shop and sometimes furnished apartments on a rental basis. Some tenants in the building here used his furniture.

"Come, we'll show you—"

Silent, beaten down, the landlord plodded ahead to open the doors on the rented furniture.

So now I had moved in, with a patched but attractive antique Persian rug, a battered replica of Jefferson's imposing desk, and a pair of cherry endtables, one supposedly from the old Bloomingdale farm. Long before these items were dragged up the narrow stairs I had hung up my cowboy hat against the newly painted wall, plain off-white, no pink, no roses. Under the hat I tacked one of the combination bullet molds and reloading tools that my father had used in his gun repair. With the roses gone there was wall space for other things too, a Sioux painting (an allegorical picture copied from one of their sacred lodges) and for a wall-sized map on which I had been working for twenty years recording the movements of the Plains Indians as fast as I could verify their camps and trails. By the time I had the map up, I knew a little more about the New Yorker's notion of speed and tried to control my western impatience as I waited for the telephone and the gas to be connected. When the man from Con Edison finally came he tinkered around the stove and particularly the ancient gas refrigerator, turning, twisting, pounding and scraping while I hovered around uneasily, listening to the man's impatient grunts and complaints.

At last he looked up. "I just figured out what's with them old fixtures here," he said. "They ain't been used since the double murder."

"Murder here? When?"

"I don't remember—'bout four years ago. Gas ain't been turned on since."

When the man was gone I searched everywhere for possible blood stains to show to my friends but the floor had been so thoroughly sanded and waxed that I could not hope for anything more incriminating than a few burned spots. I liked to imagine that the murders were tied in with the pink paneling and the roses, lost under the thick new paint, as well as the floor-to-ceiling shelves set up to hold my books. Some of the green tile had been knocked out of the bathroom wall, with other squares broken and cracked, but I couldn't reconstruct a decent bludgeoning there, not with the room almost too narrow for a good swing with a hammer or even a milk bottle, the lethal weapon in a going murder trial.

When my telephone was finally installed it proved to be the only one listed in the building, and almost at once I heard from the local draft board. I laughed, thinking it was just another case of a little knowledge of French being a dangerous thing—someone mistaking my first name, Mari, the old Swiss version of Mary, for the masculine *mari*, husband, in French. But the draft board wasn't after me, nor any of my connections, all out in the cow country or in the service. The board sought some man with an Italian name that I did not know. I explained that I just got

the telephone and that they must want an earlier subscriber.
Patiently the man went over the whole thing again, and
added that they were trying to locate a draft dodger. Perhaps I had met him or heard of him because his grandmother, Mrs. B—— lived in the building.

I did recall seeing her name on a buzzer downstairs and
had said "Good morning" to a woman at the mailbox, a
woman tiny enough to stand under my outstretched arm,
a wrinkled little old foreigner very much like my mother,
except that she had spoken with a German-Swiss accent
instead of this woman's Italian.

"That's Mrs. B——," the man from the draft board was
saying in my ear. "Call her to the telephone."

When I hesitated he pointed out that there was a war on,
his voice suggesting that I was deliberately impeding the
war effort. I went down to the woman's little back apartment and tapped on the door. She opened it and exclaimed
her welcome for the new one upstairs in her broken English. I thanked her but added that I could not come in now.
"There's a man on my telephone who wants to talk to
you."

Instantly she seemed to lose all facility for the English
language, at least as I spoke it, and while I made motions
that I hoped indicated the telephone and someone speaking, she stood with the unresponsiveness of a small person
in a bullying world, shaking her head stubbornly, saying
something rapidly in Italian that I assumed meant she did
not understand. I finally got her to come, half-dragging
her up the stairs by an elbow. She took the receiver
gingerly from my hand and shouted "Allo!" several times
and then spoke in her quick Bari Italian. This went on for
some time, the woman repeating the same explosive words
until finally she hung up.

"I go home," she said.

This happened several times until finally I pretended to

the men of the draft board that I was my secretary and knew nobody in the house. Further, I had no right to call any stranger into the apartment of my employer. By then I had heard more stories about the elusive grandson, stories unrelated to draft dodging. The little woman never mentioned him as we became casual, mildly humorous acquaintances, with faint jokes about her little-girl proportions and about my immense height (I'm scarcely tall in my home region). Because I was so *be-eg* I changed the light bulbs for my little friend or hauled down boxes and bundles from the high shelves for her. In addition I threaded her needles, always a dozen or so before I left for the west. She liked a lazy tailor's length of thread in each—at least a yard and a half or two yards, perhaps double the distance between her hands with her arms wide-stretched. Who could say when I would return?

It was true that for five, perhaps even eight months a year I was away, and my apartment became a sort of dumping ground for mail that could not hope to catch up with me as I wandered around my home region and moved from one historical repository to another, or from site to site, from Indian Reservation to old soldiers' home to early settlement. While I was away the little Italian woman kept a sharp eye out for my packages left in the downstairs hall. To anyone inquiring she insisted that I would be back soon, maybe on the day. She enjoyed her little trick and besides, it was not good to have it known that an apartment was left unattended. Apparently she was right. Several in the building were rifled while the owners were gone no more than a day or so. During all my travels nothing was ever touched in my New York apartment. Everything that I lost was pilfered while I was there—little western items sneaked out by poor routine-ridden souls who sought their secondhand adventures in Buffalo Bill or Wild Bill Hickok.

The floor below my apartment was occupied by an osteopathic physician with such diverse patients and friends as Sidney Blackmer, Marlene Dietrich, and Johnnie Lee; Elliott Nugent, Countess Tolstoy, Bil Baird, and Eleanor Roosevelt. The gallant, gregarious doctor and his lovely blonde wife, the daughter of a Ringling Brothers bandmaster, entertained frequently. Their parties were usually a mixture of the unusual and the chic from business, fashion, interior decorating, music, the dance and the stage, radio, television, and moving pictures. Sometimes I was invited. If the holidays caught me in New York I tried to pretend that I was in the west, Denver, for instance, with the old progressive New Year's gatherings, the guests looking in on half a dozen places. Perhaps I started out somewhere in Brooklyn and got back to the apartment house around two in the morning by way of several stops in Manhattan, east side and west. If the neighbors below me were having a party I usually went in to practice my one parlor trick—fortune telling. Often most of the guests thought I was part of the paid entertainment. The people from the theater always seemed most interested in even a spurious peek into the year ahead, particularly after the usual holiday toasts, although the doctor's suave and Slavic diplomacy helped his guests avoid any regrettable extreme. He did enjoy overhearing an occasional bit of what passes for confidences on New Year's Eve, and I tried to keep the fortunes light and amusing but sometimes there was a momentary glimpse into a hopelessly desperate hope that I could help recapture the long lost, or the never attained.

My apartment was within whooping distance of the excellent Circle in the Square theater and Café Society Downtown, and only three, four doors beyond a bar where some of the farther-out Village musicians got together for three A.M. jam sessions, but the row of old houses

opposite my window was a thousand miles from these in
spirit. On warm days many of the windows were occupied
by Italian women leaning on pillows spread on the sills.
They watched their children playing noisily in the narrow
street below and visited and gossiped pleasantly, or called
down to the coal oil man pushing his cart along the street,
and then vanished for the containers to carry the kerosene
back for their stoves and heaters in the old cold-water
flats.

Sometimes a murmur of people, of an expectant and
excited crowd rose from the street. After several such occasions I knew what I would see from the window—a thick
mass of people, some men and children among the women,
the faces warm and welcoming, all turned to look along
the packed little street to a black car that moved slowly
along, like the dark shiny nose of an otter swimming up a
choppy stream. The car that attracted such a crowd was
always Mrs. Roosevelt's, bringing her to Greenwich
House in one of her many activities.

I saw the same people jammed into a larger space, into
the four blocks of Washington Square, their number aug-
mented by quieter, non-Italians the day that President
Roosevelt came to Greenwich Village in the campaign
for a third term. The Square was a humming, pushing
mass of people, and as the President's car neared the Arch,
the faces lifted, an outgoing glow of love and hope on
very many, and some concern. I was reminded of another
day, when I had come to the Square early in the morning
for a little sense of space, a little open sky to ease my home-
sickness for the Plains. Near the magnificent old tree in the
northwest corner, Mrs. Roosevelt was walking Fala, the
little Scottie sniffing his way around as intently as though
in some great ancestral hunt. A man cut across from the
street, directly into the path of Mrs. Roosevelt. As he
passed, his head shot forward and he spit in her direction.

Fala stopped, ears up, but his mistress never broke her stride, her face unchanged.

Life is a curious complexity of switching back and forth, of echoes and re-echoes, retracings, and repetitions. As I stood there in the gray morning light I recalled our little grandmother's admonition against spitting. Sharply, in her Schaffhauser dialect, she reminded us, *"Da Teufel spucht; d' Engel seht's nit."*

Each time that I returned to the little stub of Village street there were changes: fewer Italian women with their pleasant gossip, their loud and threatening calls down to their laggard children, more of the windows discreetly blinded and curtained. Once in August I had to come into town for a couple of hot, unhappy weeks to finish an over-due book. Although there were fewer Italians around, the windows across from me were open, one of them com-pletely unshaded, the lamps inside blazing afternoon and night. I had moved my typewriter to a window where I could get a little breeze and catch a diagonal glimpse of 59 Grove Street where Tom Paine lived and died. Think-ing of him was a sort of comfort during my concern with the increasing complexity of the post-war world that I had been trying to capture in an allegory. After some time I became aware that I had been staring straight ahead, across into the open window and at a young woman completely nude preparing dinner, the thin-shanked man digging in the refrigerator as nude as she. They had gone about their tasks of kitchen and table so unselfconsciously that I had not realized their nakedness.

Embarrassed, I moved my work, and a few days later the tabloids carried a picture of an "oriental" dancer in costume, from the picture surely involved in some scandal that could not interest me. I was turning the page when the address leapt out at me—the house across the street, and now I recognized the young woman I had seen cooking in the nude, with a photograph of a man who was being sued for divorce by his wife, apparently over the dancer. I could not be certain that this was the thin-shanked individual I had seen. Plainly a man's pants are a better disguise than a jeweled bra and harem skirt-trousers slung below the navel are for a woman. But it was really the address that had identified the dancer and possibly this was not the man I had seen. There could have been several.

Café Society Downtown was an occasional diversion for all of us with windows on the street. My bedroom was an inside one, with only an air shaft and casement windows that opened into the living room. Even so, on warm nights I could hear the commotion around Café Society at closing time. Once I sat on the fire escape to watch two dinner-jacketed men take punches at each other outside the Café's door, loose, awkward punches, slip-footed and wavering. One of the men flailed his arms around until a crescent of white burst at the back of one arm hole and then on the other. Evidently one of the punches landed, at least his opponent went down, and when the bystanders managed to get the man to his feet, blood was running in dark streaks down his shirt front. By next morning someone had placed a bench over the patch of dried blood to protect it from any casual shower of rain and the wear of passing feet. In the papers there was a report of another Errol Flynn brawl.

Later there were stories of a more serious slugging there. I had heard rumors that a strong-arm gang was ordering all Negroes out of the Village after eleven at night. One morning the drug store where we gathered for our coffee breaks buzzed with news about the Café. The management featured colored artists like Billie Holiday and Pearl Primus but now it seemed that two young Negro women waiting in a taxicab for one of the singers at the Downtown had been dragged from the cab and beaten up so they had to be taken to a hospital. There was a glum nodding among the coffee drinkers. Just another attack by the gang of young hoodlums of the white-supremacy stripe that had been operating around the Village since the war.

Apparently this was one more change brought by the departure of LaGuardia. The little Mrs. B—— with the draft-dodging grandson had been one of the first to regret the mayor's decision not to run again. I had noticed an undercurrent of nervousness in her protests when I went west, something besides the usual pretense in the stricken look when she saw my suitcases at the curb, something absentminded.

"You go!" she cried accusingly, as though I were deserting her to flood or prairie fire or Indian raid, but still laughing a little underneath. And when I returned she greeted me like a long lost cousin from Puglia. "You come-a back, you son-um-gum!" she shouted to me across Seventh Avenue, much to the amusement of the good Italians gathered out in front of the Tamawa Club sign.

But she had nothing more to say and two days later the little old woman tapped on my door and came in, wiping her eyes in the shamed way of small European women— the way my mother and her mother did, always needing to hide their tears. This looked serious and I got Mrs. B—— settled on the sofa and tried to think of something to divert her, for obviously open comforting wouldn't do and none of our little jokes seemed appropriate. Finally she told me. Since the mayor announced he would not run again, her grandson and his gang planned to move back into town.

"All time they got stay in Jersey," she said. But now sometime (meaning soon) they would come back. Her grandson, he a disgrace. She would not stay to be shamed. She would go to a niece in Brooklyn, not come back.

I tried to reassure her as well as I could but she was determined to accept no comfort. She sniffled secretly all the way down the stairs and while I climbed on a chair to lift her old suitcases and boxes from the shelf. The next morning she was gone. I never saw her again.

The life across the street from me changed more and more rapidly, with venetian blinds in many windows where the Italian women had leaned on their pillows, a fine big boxer standing in one, the dog looking down upon the street for hours, his magnificent eyes somehow sad. Then one night I was awakened by a pistol shot, and a second one. I threw on a robe and ran out to a front window. Crouching down below the sill, I peered into an open lighted window across from me. Under the half-drawn shade, I could see the body of a man on the floor, feet toward me, and the lower portions of two people, a woman in something long and maroon moving frantically back and forth and a man in dark trousers standing with his back toward me. There were more shots, apparently fired by the man I could see. One bullet, perhaps aimed downward, hit a hard surface and with the ricochetting whine that I knew very well, it struck the window above me. The bullet was well spent and made only a small hole, sending a chip of glass down upon my head. For a moment I was right back in the cattleman-settler troubles of my childhood.

I never tried to check on that possible double murder in my apartment all the fifteen years that my cowboy hat hung on the wall, though the gas man had sounded very definite. The little hole in the window on the fourth floor was there long after I moved my outpost.

A SANDOZ CHRONOLOGY

CHECKLIST OF
MARI SANDOZ'S WRITING

ACKNOWLEDGMENTS

A SANDOZ CHRONOLOGY

The parents of Mari Sandoz, Jules Ami Sandoz and Mary Elizabeth Fehr, his fourth wife, were both born in Switzerland, Jules Sandoz in Neuchatel in 1857 and Mary Elizabeth Fehr nine years later in Schaffhausen. As a young man, Jules Sandoz studied medicine in Zurich. After a quarrel with his family he came to America in 1881 and to western Nebraska in 1884, bringing with him his dream of building communities which would have political and economic freedom. He located colonists on homesteads in the Niobrara country, inducing them to immigrate and settle there with his descriptions of how the virgin land could be developed. "As soon as the region was fairly well tamed, his taste for conflict made him restless and he turned to the frontier of experimentation in fruit and soothed his turbulent spirit in fights with his neighbors. He was a frontiersman who opened the way for the pioneers who lived with him" (Mari Sandoz to Mamie J. Meredith, n.d., 1936).

In the following chronology, all first-person quotations are from "Autobiographical Sketch of Mari Sandoz' Early Years," in *Hostiles and Friendlies: Selected Short Writings of Mari Sandoz* (Lincoln: University of Nebraska Press, 1959), pp. xv–xxi.

1896   Birth of Mari Sandoz, eldest of the six children of Jules and Mary Elizabeth Sandoz, on the Sandoz homestead in Sheridan County.

1905   "I was about nine when I started to school and made the wonderful discovery that little black marks were the key to wonderful stories. . . . Father came from an upper-middle-class professional family. He didn't believe in fiction. That was for the hired girl and the hired man. So I had to borrow books and smuggle them into the

house in the sloppy front of our low-belted dresses. . . .
I started writing when I started to school. . . . I spoke
only a few words of hybrid English at the time, with an
equal smattering of Polish and French mixed into my
mother tongue, Swiss-German."

1906   " When I was ten I decided to write a story—secretly, of
course—and submit it to a newspaper offering a book
as a prize. It was published but it didn't get first prize. . . .
But when it came home I found out that I belonged to a
family that not only did not read fiction, but certainly
did not write it. Father put me in a cellar. I believed that
when a parent went to the trouble of punishing a child,
the least the child could do was act punished. I howled
to high heaven. I knew there were snakes in the cellar.
I also knew they were harmless. After some time Father
came along and asked if I wanted to go quail hunting.
I sure did. . . . After that I used a pen name."

1912   "By sixteen I had gone to school [four and a half years],
passed the rural teachers' examination, and had a school."
In all, Mari Sandoz taught seven years in country schools.

1922   "I decided that I must have a college education. I came
to Lincoln and sat around in the anterooms of various
deans for two weeks between conferences with advisers
who insisted that I must go to high school. Finally bushy-
haired Dean Sealock got tired of seeing me waiting and
said, 'Well, you can't do any more than fail—' and
registered me [on June 5, 1922]."

1922–1932 "I worked here and there, attended University as
I could, wrote seventy-eight short stories (and didn't sell
one), won honorable mention in a Harper's Intercol-
legiate Contest in 1926, and wrote a bad novel that,
fortunately, no one would publish. . . . I worked my way
in the University by afternoon jobs, one and a half years
in a drug laboratory and one and a half years as an English
assistant, and the rest of the time four hours a day in the
State Historical Society in research and nights on the

proof desk of the *State Journal.*" In January 1927 Mari Sandoz's short story "The Vine" appeared in the first issue of *Prairie Schooner*, and from 1927 to 1929 she was associate editor of *School Executives Magazine.* (She is listed on the masthead under her married name, Marie S. Macumber, which she used at this time.)

In the mid-twenties Mari Sandoz began work on *Old Jules.* "Early I saw that Old Jules and his community were by far the most promising material in my experience. As I worked with the material, three years in research and two in the writing, it gradually dawned on me that here was a character who embodied not only his own strengths and weaknesses but those of all humanity —that his struggles were universal struggles and his defeats at the hands of his environment and his own insufficiencies were those of mankind; his tenacious clinging to his dream the symbol of man's undying hope that over the next hill he will find the green pastures of his desire."

1933–1935 "The ms [of *Old Jules*] was in most of the larger publishing houses in America. . . . In 1933, after eight rejections, I submitted it in the Atlantic contest. When it was returned with a curt rejection letter, I quit." Before she left Lincoln, Mari Sandoz burned eighty-five stories. "Starved out, my confidence in even my critical faculties gone, I gave up writing permanently and sneaked back to the sandhills. . . . But in less than a month I was building myself a shack of privacy in which to write a novel that I had been thinking about doing for nine or ten years. It was *Slogum House.* By the time the rough draft was done, I was offered more work at the State Historical Society in Lincoln. I made a new copy of *Old Jules* and started it on its alphabetical round of publishers again. On its fourteenth trip out it was accepted—and won the Atlantic nonfiction prize in 1935." [For the publication dates of Mari Sandoz's books and short writings, see the checklist on pp. 161–165, below.]

1941 On staff of Writers Conference, University of Colorado.

1943   January. Takes an apartment in New York.

1946   On staff of Writers Conference, University of Indiana.

1947–1956   In charge of Advanced Novel Writing, Writers Institute, Eight Weeks Summer Session, University of Wisconsin.

1950   Honorary degree, University of Nebraska. "Doctor of Literature: Mari Sandoz, distinguished Nebraska historian, biographer, novelist, story writer, authority on Indians of the Nebraska territory and neighboring states. Published two books of a six-volume study of the trans-Missouri country. Author of three novels and many stories of Nebraska frontier life. Winner of the Atlantic nonfiction award. Recognized nationally as a representative midwest writer: cited for contributions to the Saga of Crazy Horse and other Indian history. Widely-known teacher in creative writing at several state universities."

1954   August 23: Mari Sandoz Day in Nebraska. "WHEREAS, the indomitable pioneer spirit has been typical of Nebraskans since the first settlement of this State, and WHEREAS, we Nebraskans are extremely proud of our fine heritage left to us by our pioneering forefathers, and WHEREAS, a native Nebraskan, Mari Sandoz, has immortalized the spirit and history of Nebraska and the Midwest by her writings, NOW, THEREFORE, I, Robert B. Crosby, as Governor of the State of Nebraska, do hereby proclaim August 23, 1954, as MARI SANDOZ DAY."

September 23: Received the Nebraska Native Sons and Daughters Award for Distinguished Achievement—the first such award made.

Crazy Horse named one of the Ten Best Serious Books of the West.

1955   National Achievement Award, The Westerners, Chicago Corral. "In recognition of her contribution to the preservation of the cultural background of the American West through her writing, and for her unequalled achievement in having four of her books selected by Westerners in a nationwide poll as ranking in the One Hundred Best Books on the West, this award is unanimously conferred by the Chicago Corral of The Westerners. Given this nineteenth day of December, One Thousand Nine Hundred and Fifty-Five. HERBERT O. BRAYER, President; L. P. JERRARD, Secretary."

1957 Headliner Award, Theta Sigma Phi.

1958 Made a life member of the Nebraska State Historical Society. Annual Buffalo Award, The Westerners, New York Corral.

1961 Western Heritage Award of National Cowboy Hall of Fame.

1963 Spur Award of Western Writers of America for best western juvenile, *The Story Catcher*.

Levi Strauss Golden Saddleman Award for best western novel, *The Story Catcher*.

1964 With the publication of *The Beaver Men: Spearheads of Empire*, Mari Sandoz completes her masterwork, the Great Plains series. The six volumes of the series, in the order of their historical chronology, are: *The Beaver Men*, *Crazy Horse*, *Cheyenne Autumn*, *The Buffalo Hunters*, *The Cattlemen*, and *Old Jules*.

1965 Erection of Mari Sandoz Hall at the University of Nebraska.

1966 March 10. Death of Mari Sandoz in New York City.

1968 Dedication of Mari Sandoz Historical Marker in Sheridan County, Nebraska.

CHECKLIST OF
MARI SANDOZ'S WRITING

This checklist was corrected by Mari Sandoz up through 1959. When date of composition of a work is known, it is listed directly after the title. The works are listed in order of composition rather than of publication. Book reviews and newspaper articles are not included.

FEARBITTEN. 1925.
> Short story. Honorable mention, Harper's Intercollegiate Short Story Contest, 1926. Unpublished.

THE VINE. 1925.
> Short story. Signed Marie Macumber. *Prairie Schooner.* January 1927.

OLD POTATO FACE. 1926.
> Short story. Signed Marie Macumber. *Prairie Schooner.* January 1928.

DUMB CATTLE. 1926.
> Short story. Signed Marie Macumber. *Prairie Schooner.* January 1929.

THE SMART MAN. 1928.
> Short story. *Prairie Schooner.* Spring 1959.

THE KINKAIDER COMES AND GOES. 1929.
> Article. *North American Review.* April and May 1930.

SANDHILL SUNDAYS. 1930
> Article. *Folksay: A Regional Miscellany*, ed. B. A. Botkin. Norman: University of Oklahoma Press, 1931.

WHAT SHOULD BE CONSIDERED WHEN CHOOSING A PROFESSION? 1932.
> Essay. Signed Marie Macumber. *Daily Nebraskan*, April 3, 1932.

PIECES TO A QUILT. 1932.
> Short story. *North American Review*. May 1933.

MUSKY, THE NARRATIVE OF A MUSKRAT. 1932.
> Article. *Nature*. November 1933.

OLD JULES. 1927–1933.
> Biography. Atlantic Nonfiction Prize, 1935. Boston: Little, Brown & Co., 1935.

WHITE METEOR. 1933.
> Short story. *Ladies' Home Journal*. January 1937.

PIONEER WOMEN. 1934.
> Article. Written for the Fremont Women's Club. Unpublished. Excerpts quoted in *Hostiles and Friendlies* (see below).

THE BIRDMAN. 1934–1935.
> Indian tale. Omaha *Sunday World-Herald Magazine*. February 10, 1935.

RIVER POLAK. 1935.
> Short story. *Atlantic Monthly*. September 1937.

I WROTE A BOOK. 1935.
> Article. *Nebraska Alumnus*. November 1935.

THE NEW FRONTIER WOMAN. 1935–1936.
> Article. *Country Gentleman*. September 1936.

MIST AND THE TALL WHITE TOWER. 1936.
> Short story. *Story*. September 1936.

STAY HOME, YOUNG WRITER. 1937.
> Article. *The Quill*. June 1937.

SLOGUM HOUSE. 1933–1937.
> Novel. Boston: Little, Brown & Co. 1937.

THE DEVIL'S LANE. 1937–1938.
> Short story. *Ladies' Home Journal*. April 1938.

THE GIRL IN THE HUMBERT. 1938–1939.
> Short story. *Saturday Evening Post*. March 4, 1939.

BONE JOE AND THE SMOKIN' WOMAN. 1938–1939.
> Novelette. *Scribner's Magazine*. March 1939.

FAR LOOKER. 1939.
> Indian tale. *The Sight-Giver*. February 1939.

CAPITAL CITY. 1939.
> Novel. Boston: Little, Brown & Co., 1939.

PEACHSTONE BASKET. 1939.
>   Short story. *Prairie Schooner*. Fall 1943.

CRAZY HORSE: THE STRANGE MAN OF THE OGLALAS. 1942
>   Biography. New York: Alfred A. Knopf, Inc. 1942.

ANYBODY CAN WRITE. 1943.
>   Article. *The Writer*. April 1944.

SIT YOUR SADDLE SOLID. 1944.
>   Short story. *Saturday Evening Post*. February 10, 1945.

THE SPIKE-EARED DOG. 1945.
>   Short story. *Saturday Evening Post*. August 11, 1945.

MARTHA OF THE YELLOW BRAIDS. 1945.
>   Article. *Prairie Schooner*. Summer 1947.

THE NEIGHBOR. 1945.
>   Article. *Prairie Schooner*. Winter 1956.

THE TOM-WALKER. 1947.
>   Novel. New York: The Dial Press, Inc., 1947.

YULETIDE SAGA OF A LONE TREE. 1947.
>   Allegory. Philadelphia *Inquirer Book Review Supplement*. December 7, 1947.

THE LOST SITTING BULL. 1949.
>   Article. Published as: "There Were Two Sitting Bulls." *Blue Book*. November 1949.

THE LOST SCHOOL BUS. 1950–1951.
>   Novelette. *Saturday Evening Post*. May 19, 1951.

WINTER THUNDER. 1950–1951.
>   Unabridged version of "The Lost School Bus." Philadelphia: Westminster Press, 1954.

THE SON. 1951.
>   Article. Published as: "What the Sioux Taught Me." *Reader's Digest*. May 1952. Reprinted from *Empire*. February 24, 1952.

CHEYENNE AUTUMN. 1952.
>   Biography. New York: McGraw-Hill, 1955.

MISS MORISSA: DOCTOR OF THE GOLD TRAIL. 1952–1953.
>   Novel. New York: McGraw-Hill, 1955.

THE INDIAN LOOKS AT HIS FUTURE. 1954.
>   Article. *Family Weekly*. April 11, 1954.

THE BUFFALO HUNTERS: THE STORY OF THE HIDE MEN. 1954.
> History. New York: Hastings House, 1954.

THE SEARCH FOR THE BONES OF CRAZY HORSE. 1954.
> Article. *The Westerners' Brand Book.* New York Posse. Autumn 1954.

LOOK OF THE WEST—1854. 1954.
> Article. *Nebraska History.* December 1954.

SOME ODDITIES OF THE AMERICAN INDIAN. 1954.
> Article. *The Westerners' Brand Book.* Denver Posse. 1955.

ACCEPTANCE SPEECH, DISTINGUISHED ACHIEVEMENT AWARD. 1955.
> *The Westerners' Brand Book.* Chicago Corral. January 1956.

NEBRASKA. 1956.
> Article. *Holiday.* May 1956.

DECEMBER 2006 A.D. 1956.
> Article. Unpublished. Enclosed in the cornerstone of KETV, Omaha, Nebraska, to be opened in fifty years.

THE HORSECATCHER. 1956.
> Novel. Philadelphia: Westminster Press, 1957.

THE CATTLEMEN: FROM THE RIO GRANDE ACROSS THE FAR MARIAS. 1957–1958.
> History. New York: Hastings House, 1958.

TYRANT OF THE PLAINS.
> Article. Adaptation of a section of *The Cattlemen. Saturday Evening Post.* June 7, 1958.

HOSTILES AND FRIENDLIES: SELECTED SHORT WRITINGS OF MARI SANDOZ. 1925–1955.
> Short stories, articles, a novelette. Lincoln: University of Nebraska Press, 1959.

SON OF THE GAMBLIN' MAN: THE YOUTH OF AN ARTIST.
> Novel. New York: Clarkson N. Potter, Inc. 1960.

LOOK OF THE LAST FRONTIER.
> Article. *American Heritage.* June 1961.

THESE WERE THE SIOUX.
> Nonfiction. New York: Hastings House, 1961.

LOVE SONG TO THE PLAINS.
> Nonfiction. New York: Harper & Row, 1961.

FLY SPECK BILLIE'S CAVE.
>In *Legends and Tales of the Old West*, ed. S. Omar Barker.
>New York: Doubleday & Company, Inc., 1962.

THE BUFFALO SPRING CAVE.
>In *Legends and Tales of the Old West,* ed. S. Omar Barker.
>New York: Doubleday & Company, Inc., 1962.

OUTPOST IN NEW YORK. 1962.
>Article. *Prairie Schooner.* Summer 1963.

THE HOMESTEAD IN PERSPECTIVE. 1962.
>Article. Collected in *Land Use Policy and Problems in the United States*, ed. Howard W. Ottoson. Lincoln: University of Nebraska Press, 1963.

INTRODUCTION to *The Cheyenne Indians: Their History and Ways of Life* by George Bird Grinnell. July 1962.
>New York: Cooper Square Publishers, Inc., 1962.

THE STORY CATCHER.
>Novel. Philadelphia: Westminster Press, 1963.

THE BEAVER MEN: SPEARHEADS OF EMPIRE.
>History. New York: Hastings House, 1964.

OLD JULES COUNTRY: A SELECTION FROM OLD JULES AND THIRTY YEARS OF WRITING SINCE THE BOOK WAS PUBLISHED.
>Includes the following previously uncollected pieces: "Evening Song" (Cheyenne chant) and two articles, "Coyotes and Eagles" and "Snakes." New York: Hastings House, 1965.

THE BATTLE OF THE LITTLE BIG HORN. 1965.
>History. Philadelphia: J. B. Lippincott Co., 1966.

THE CHRISTMAS OF THE PHONOGRAPH RECORDS. 1965.
>Recollection. Lincoln: University of Nebraska Press, 1966

THE AMOS BAD HEART BULL PICTURE HISTORY. 1965.
>Introduction to *A Pictographic History of the Oglala Sioux.* Lincoln: University of Nebraska Press, 1967.

N.B. A number of Mari Sandoz's letters have appeared in the Gordon (Nebraska) Journal, *prepared for publication by her sister Caroline Sandoz Pifer.*

ACKNOWLEDGMENTS

The University of Nebraska Press wishes to express its thanks to the Sandoz Family Corporation for permission to reprint the articles collected in this book. We are particularly grateful to Caroline Sandoz Pifer for the loan of letters, manuscripts, and other materials; for checking the chronology and bibliography; and for the interest she has taken in this project from its inception. We also wish to thank Joseph Svoboda, University of Nebraska Archivist and curator of the Sandoz Collection, for information about various awards to Mari Sandoz.

DATE DUE

PRINTED IN U.S.A.